T0330452

Resolving the Crisis in Research by Changing the Game

GAME CHANGERS AND GROUND BREAKERS

This series is an important forum for leading academics to envisage an alternative future for business schools and academia in general. The series is open to those who have something interesting to say on academic impact and relevance, academic and teaching assessment systems, the direction of business schools and the future of universities. Books in this series may be controversial or brave and will be insightful in pointing the ahead way for scholars, business schools and universities.

Resolving the Crisis in Research by Changing the Game

An Ecosystem and a Sharing Philosophy

Morten Huse

Professor of Organisation and Management, BI Norwegian Business School, Norway

GAME CHANGERS AND GROUND BREAKERS

Edward Elgar
PUBLISHING

Cheltenham, UK • Northampton, MA, USA

© Morten Huse 2020

All rights reserved. No part of this publication may be reproduced, stored in a
retrieval system or transmitted in any form or by any means, electronic, mechanical or
photocopying, recording, or otherwise without the prior permission of the publisher.

Published by
Edward Elgar Publishing Limited
The Lypiatts
15 Lansdown Road
Cheltenham
Glos GL50 2JA
UK

Edward Elgar Publishing, Inc.
William Pratt House
9 Dewey Court
Northampton
Massachusetts 01060
USA

A catalogue record for this book
is available from the British Library

Library of Congress Control Number: 2019956673

This book is available electronically in the **Elgar**online
Business subject collection
DOI 10.4337/9781789906646

ISBN 978 1 78990 663 9 (cased)
ISBN 978 1 78990 664 6 (eBook)

Printed and bound by CPI Group (UK) Ltd, Croydon CR0 4YY

Contents

Preface and acknowledgments: Introspection and *Ritorno al Passato*

This book is about resolving the crisis in research. I am addressing urgent topics in most academic disciplines, but with a focus on social sciences. However, my experiences are mostly from management research, and most of my examples are thus related to management scholarship. The book builds on reflections about my experiences from the past, but returning to the past may be a good starting point for setting the direction for the future. *Ritorno al passato* is a restaurant in Rome. I used this restaurant as my office during the seven years in which I worked in Rome monthly. I have many positive memories from this restaurant. There, I felt that I was at the center of the world. I was living in my busy reality at the beginning of the twenty-first century, while my table and chair in the restaurant were located in such a way that I could see directly into the Pantheon. Two thousand years ago the Pantheon was the center of the world. The dome of the Pantheon was the largest dome in the world for 1300 years, and is still the largest unsupported dome. Pantheon means "honor all gods," and the Pantheon was completed in its present shape by the emperor Hadrian, probably dedicated about 126 AD. This was the golden age of the Roman empire, which the Pantheon represented. It was a true testament to the might and glory of a worldly government. The Pantheon represents a true cultural revolution.

In my office in front of the Pantheon, I saw the movements of politicians, business people, tourists, homeless people, and all the colleagues and friends that came to see me. I had time for reflection and writing, discussions with strangers, sharing experiences with my students and friends, and experiencing the joy of a good wine. In *Ritorno al passato* I was able to reflect on what matters most, about Socrates and dialogues, and the importance of the heart and passion. I am thus dedicating this book to *Ritorno al passato* even though I also argue this book is about creating a new game. This game was illustrated through the sharing, communal, open, and impact-driven philosophy that was formulated as I was sitting in my office in front of the Pantheon.

I am committed to resolving the crisis in research through my scholarship. My contribution, and this book, are influenced by introspection. In practice this means that I am interpreting the reality through reflecting on my previous experiences. They are shaping my understandings and position. I thus write this book in a personal way with an "I form." However, my experiences and my passions become more evident as we move from Part I to Part II. I am writing about something I believe in and that is very close to my heart.

This book is a spinoff from and a development of an ERC Advanced grant proposal I submitted in 2017, and it leans on my research trajectory. The book is the result of a journey of at least 40 years, and I use examples that have a history dating back more than 40 years. In this period, I have integrated research, practice, and policymaking. Johanna Degen has been my tutor and inspirational partner in introspection. Hannah Möltner and Alessandra Rigolini stimulated me to reflect on experiences that led to a "sharing philosophy" that is communal, open, and impact-driven. I am very thankful for this inspiration.

My initial research education came in the 1970s, and throughout most of the 1980s I worked in business. In 1989, I returned to academia. I was not a scout as a child, but I often describe my values as those of a scout. Justice and fairness are important, and I have always been willing to fight for what I believe in. Sometimes, this has brought me trouble, and I got many bruises. I have also accepted that I cannot be friends with everybody or expect that everybody will like me. I have enemies, and I am sure that not everybody will be happy with what I write in this book. Nevertheless, the reason why I write it is that I believe in it and want to do something that is good for business, for society, and for academia.

Twice in the 1990s I was taken to hospital by ambulance. In both cases the outcome could have been fatal. I learned from these experiences that "life is too short to drink bad wine," that is, that I do not have time to do things which are not important. Further, I do not have time to spend with people that simply take my energy. I should spend time with people who give energy. This book reflects both aspects—that of importance and that of people.

For many years I persistently voiced an overall criticism of the "publish or perish" culture in academia. I was thinking of myself along the lines of Cato in the old Roman senate. He persistently advocated for the total destruction of Cartago, and repeatedly stated "Carthago delenda est" (Cartago must be destroyed). The core message in this book is something that I have communicated regularly and repeatedly since the mid-1990s. The "publish or perish" culture, with its "lamp" and "hammer" syndromes, is moving us away from doing important, relevant, and venturesome research (Huse, 1996). I have had an interesting academic journey since the mid-1990s, but I have been like Cato, and I am still repeating it: "Carthago delenda est." That is what this book is about.

Over the years, I developed increasing recognition as a scholar. My stubborn insistence that Cartago must be destroyed (that we must fight the "publish or perish" culture) has given me many bruises, but also led to many experiences and lessons. I have also had opportunities to influence. I was a member of the board of governors of the International Association of Business Society (IABS) 1966–99 and President of the European Academy of Management (EURAM – presented in Chapter 4) 2010–12, and while writing this book I was elected as a member of the board of governors at the Academy of Management (AOM – presented in Chapter 3) for the 2019–22 period. The Norefjell workshops (Chapter 6), the Witten seminars (Chapter 7), and the Women on Board Cruise Workshops (Chapter 8) have also given me opportunities to influence.

On the practitioner side, for example, I was President of the National Association of Directors in Norway 1997–2000 and a member of the Catalyst Europe advisory board 2009–14. At the same time, I held full- or part-time positions at academic institutions in several countries. I have been living and working in the intersection between research and practice, but always bringing my scholarly identity with me. These experiences contributed to framing and writing this book. In practice, this means that I do not only criticize; I also bring suggestions for solutions to the table.

In 2018, I had a book published in the Cambridge Elements series (Huse, 2018a). That was a provocative book about value-creating boards. However, Amedeo Pugliese challenged me to be even more provocative, also considering methods. The 2018 book was not about methods, but this book is about method. Amedeo made me channel my methodological sentiments into the present book. Several friends and colleagues have contributed to this book with ideas about a "sharing philosophy." Some have given comments on the whole book, others on parts of it or possible spin-offs of the book. In addition to those previously mentioned, I will highlight in particular Thomas Clarke, Jonas Gabrielsson, Juliane Göke, Wafa Khlif, and Sibel Yamak. For discussion and encouragement, thanks are also due to Thomas Durand, Patricia Gabaldon, Benson Honig, Silke Machold, and Stella Nkomo, but also to many others whom I have met over the years who shared my sentiments. Discussions with Alessandro Zattoni over many years have been important.

One spin-off from the book is the paper "What matters most for our scholarly community: Reflections from former AOM presidents" (Huse, 2019). The AOM presidents from 1994 to 2018 were given the opportunity to comment on this paper, which reflects on Chapter 3 of this book. About half of them offered important comments, in particular Jean Bartunek, Thomas Lee, Andrew van de Ven, and Jim Walsh. My colleague here in Oslo, Susann Gjerde, also gave me important support in writing that paper. Thanks to all of them.

Thanks to Francine O'Sullivan, who immediately saw the potential in this book and encouraged me to have it published with Edward Elgar. Thanks to all those that have formed me on the journey leading to this book. Thanks for all the business people and policy activists that have joined me using action research and the Champagne method. Thanks to all my students that have patiently allowed me to experiment with, and have learned to apply, anthroposophical and Humboldtian teaching philosophy. Finally, thanks to all those, including colleagues, friends, and particularly my wife Cathinca, that have borne with me as all of my available time was taken up with writing this book.

Morten Huse
Oslo, September 2019

1. Introduction: Is scholarship in crisis?

> Our first priority must be a reorientation of social science research from the omnipresent requirement to continuously publish in "high-quality journals" to the overriding goal and purpose of creating original knowledge that matters to society.
>
> (Alvesson, Gabriel, and Paulsen, 2017: 85)

Is there a crisis in academic research? A growing number of voices are echoing a concern for the future of academia and our scholarly profession. This seems to be a worry in most disciplines, but my personal experiences come mostly from management scholarship. Management research has been subject to critical attention during recent years. There have been calls for redirection toward what matters most, and toward scholarship with an impact. In this book, I suggest a way forward.

CRISIS IN SCHOLARSHIP

The conduct of management research is the subject of increasing criticism from several perspectives and sources (Aguinis et al., 2014; Honig et al., 2017; Pettigrew, 2011; Tsui, 2013). The criticism is related to various aspects of our research institutions, message, audience, channels, and community, as well as to concerns about the future of our scholarly identity. Its importance has been addressed in recent keynote presentations at main management conferences such as, for example, the 2018 conference of the Academy of Management (AOM), the 2017 and 2019 conferences of the European Academy of Management (EURAM), and the 2017 conference of the European Group for Organizational Studies (EGOS). We have also recently seen how these issues are being addressed by movements such as the San Francisco Declaration on Research Assessment (DORA) and Responsible Research in Business and Management (RRBM), as well as national research evaluation initiatives.

I will start this book with some reflections about scholarship and what good scholarship is. My academic background is in the AOM. North American thinking about good scholarship has thus influenced me. However, I have lived and worked in Europe all my life, and during the period 2010–12, I was President of EURAM. Reflections from these experiences have urged me to write this book, and I present some here.

For several years I have listened to the criticism and concerns raised by Andrew Pettigrew and Mats Alvesson. Their many contributions have also stimulated me to raise my voice on the topic, and a few years ago my thinking was sharpened as I applied for a European Research Council (ERC) Advanced Grant. The ERC defined research excellence in terms of groundbreaking, creative and independent achievements beyond the state of the art; innovation potential; sound leadership in training and advancing young scientists; and work that has second and third-order impacts. I brought these concepts with me when writing this book.

In a long series of publications, Pettigrew and Alvesson have raised concerns regarding our profession as management scholars, and that we as management scholars are meeting neither rigor nor relevance criteria. They argue that our research often lacks meaning, reflection, and impact. Furthermore, Alvesson and Pettigrew have both discussed the future of business schools. In a recent book, Alvesson et al. (2017) search for meaning in our research, and describe the present publishing system in critical terms. They argue that research publications are escalating, but the research contains less and less meaning. Scholars are becoming publishing technicians. Alvesson et al. make distinctions among problem definitions and solutions at individual, institutional, and policy levels. They do not present one main solution or one way of solving everything, but rather offer many small messages that they argue can contribute to giving meaning. Their first point is, however, "reorientation of social science research from the omnipresent requirement to continuously publish in 'high-quality journals' to the overriding goal and purpose of creating original knowledge that matters to society" (2017: 85).

ATTACKS ON OUR SCHOLARLY ECOSYSTEM

Research should contribute to the accumulation and dissemination of knowledge to all of society. The ultimate objective should be to come up with a breakthrough that changes our lives for the better (Moosa, 2018: 173). This ideal is under attack, as is the role of our institutions, our message, our community, our channels, and our audience. These issues are all important for developing a sustainable scholarly ecosystem. An ecosystem is a concept developed to secure sustainability, and in this book I will introduce the elements in a scholarly sustainable ecosystem. The main elements in my presentation are institutions, message, audience, channels, and community. I will argue that this system may help us analyze our present status and contribute to achieving sustainability. This ecosystem may help us understand where we are today, and help us toward true and sustainable scholarship. The book is knitted around these ecosystem elements and relationships.

My main experiences are within business schools, and particularly in the field of management. Business schools face pressures that seem particularly acute (Hall and Martin, 2019). They are not necessarily more disposed to misconduct, but competitive pressure may be greater on business schools and their faculty than in many other areas. Rewards for publishing in elite journals are often more lucrative, and the research findings in business may not, in the short run, do any direct harm to business.

What is our message? Our view of scholarship has narrowed over time. Quality is today measured in terms of where and at what pace scholars are getting their work published, rather than in terms of the impact of their work. What is true scholarship? Boyer (1990) offers a benchmark reflection about what true scholarship is. Scholars are academics who conduct research, publish, and then perhaps convey their knowledge to students or apply what they have learned (Boyer, 1990: 15). Boyer argues that the functions of scholarship dynamically interact and form an interdependent whole (1990: 25).

A neoliberal market ideology is entering academia (Moosa, 2018).[1] This ideology has a focus on extrinsic monetary incentives and self-reliance. This has consequences for definitions of academic careers and what is needed to achieve them. The criteria for academic careers are vulnerable to globalization and international employment patterns. But what do we know about what constitutes a sustainable scholarly community? What does it mean to make an academic career? What types of academic careers do we have? How do we become a part of a scholarly community, and how do we serve it? My message in this book is that we need to go beyond a "publish or perish" (POP) oriented, "winner takes all" culture.

---

[1] www.theguardian.com/commentisfree/2013/jun/11/neoliberalism-hijacked-vocabulary, accessed September 16, 2019.

There is strong concern about the way we communicate our research, particularly with regard to channels. All over the world today, in every academic discipline, there is concern about a decline in the average quality of articles published in academic journals (Scott, 2019). A larger share of university and business school professors must publish to meet the survival demands of their institutions. There has thus been an increasing demand for journals in which to publish. Alvesson et al. (2017) paint a critical picture of the present academic publishing game, and present proposals and suggestions for recovering meaning in our publications. Strong concern is thus also raised about scientific misconduct in management research (Honig and Lampel, 2018; Tourish, 2019). We are experiencing an audit and surveillance culture with negative consequences (Walsh, 2011).

Research is often seen as a self-referential inward-looking system. It is often incremental and gap spotting. It is not heavily influenced by expectations of society and media, politics and business; and theory and practice are not connected. I take the position that our research should be addressed to a large set of stakeholders, and not only to a narrow set in academia.

Chapter 2 sets out the POP culture, Boyer's work on true scholarship, and the scholarly ecosystem.

ORGANIZATIONAL DEBATES AND INITIATIVES TO RESOLVING THE CRISIS

The crisis in scholarship is escalating and new, and more, actors are taking initiatives to fight this crisis and to find alternatives. For several decades, the AOM has been a leading international actor in promoting and supporting scholarship, including developing a vibrant community of scholars. The AOM has its roots in North America. It has been criticized for spreading destructive norms, but has also been a victim of larger movements. This is displayed in the reflections of many of their outgoing presidents, which have been published in the *Academy of Management Review* (AMR) since the mid-1990s The AOM presidents and the Academy's governance bodies have seen the challenges developing, but they have been like captains on a large tankship. It has been very difficult to make fast changes and to maneuver in turbulent waters away from the home ports. Reflections from the captains—the outgoing presidents of AOM—are presented in Chapter 3.

Many boats, or scholarly communities, have followed in the wake of AOM, but some have taken initiatives—either alone or together with AOM—to change the direction of the scholarly community. During my EURAM presidency in 2010–12, I had the ambition of presenting EURAM as a tugboat, supporting AOM in its navigation—including contributing with local knowledge and experiences. For this reason, we in EURAM institutionalized meetings among presidents of various associations of management. My EURAM experiences are presented in Chapter 4. EURAM is not the only association rendering resources to redirect the development of management research and scholarships— there exist several other tugboats. The British Academy of Management (BAM) has raised its voice in relation to national research assessments, several journal editors have devoted space to addressing problems in management research, and associations such as DORA and RRBM are developing to challenge topics such as the use of metrics and the lack of relevance.

The Research Evaluation Framework (REF) in the UK is a process of expert review, including assessment of outputs, impacts beyond academia, and the environment that supports research. The REF's objective is to provide a yardstick for allocation of funds. It shall provide accountability for public investment in research and produce evidence of the benefits of this investment. DORA contains a criticism of metrics-driven research evaluations. The DORA declaration requests that less emphasis is placed on publication metrics and nonarticle output is given greater inclusion. RRBM is dedicated to inspiring, encouraging, and supporting credible and useful research in the business and management disciplines. It is a virtual organization initially developed by leading management scholars from various countries. There are in addition many individual initiatives and contributions. The above mentioned initiatives will be presented in Chapter 5.

A SHARING PHILOSOPHY

My objective with this book is to contribute to creating a new game for research, not simply changing the rules of an existing one. As President of EURAM, I wanted to create a community of engaged management scholars (Huse, 2010). In this book, I will follow the call of several of the outgoing AOM presidents, for example van de Ven (2002), and present a *"sharing" philosophy* of management research. My motivation is aligned with the arguments by previous AOM presidents Jean Bartunek, Andrew van de Ven, and David Whetten that (a) *a communal*, (b) *an open source/ innovation*, and (c) *an impact-driven research philosophy* will advance the scholarship of management and may solve problems today being experienced in management research.

The *sharing philosophy* builds on concepts such as:

* *A communal approach*, including communal and joint credit; giving credit for research and not only for publications; communities of engaged scholars.
* *An open source/innovation approach*, including open sources for research, learning and innovation; leadership and liaising; venturesome research designs; holistic engagement and appreciation of diversity; appreciating impact in academia, business, and society.
* *An impact-driven approach*, including evaluating research and impact on a long-term basis; appreciated in both academia and practice; development of junior scholars; multiplicative behavioral processes.

I will try to use my experiences from various settings to present and illustrate this sharing philosophy. In Chapter 6, I will present experiences from the Norefjell workshops to illustrate the communal approach, programmatic research, and the development of "value creating board" research as a distinct research stream. In Chapter 7, I will present a lighthouse university. Witten/Herdecke University in Germany is an anthroposophical inspired private university where I spent a five-year late career period. Core lessons from Witten were open innovation and open sharing, passion and compassion, and thinking holistically, including coming close to some of our society's grand challenges. The impact-driven approach is the core of Chapter 8. It is about socially committed scholarship, longitudinal research with stakeholders, and polymorphic research.

Chapter 9 contains reflections and a discussion of how an ecosystem thinking may contribute to a move from a destructive POP culture to a culture based on true scholarship. I summarize and raise challenges on issues laid out throughout the book: what scholars are, and the scholarly life cycle; that we need more than one boat to get to true scholarship; and that we need lighthouses to help us navigate. In the final chapter, I summarize and conclude with regard to the sharing philosophy and our scholarly ecosystem. I present ways to resolve the crisis in research. Senior scholars should devote time to developing the scholarly community; scholarly associations should appreciate context-specific charges and needs; and thus we shall all stand up as lighthouses in leading academia back to true scholarship.

I wanted to write a personal book. It is provocative, and I attack the present POP culture. I want to contribute to true scholarship and a sustainable society. Across the pages, I contribute to resolving the urgent need to recover meaning in our research, and through my examples I sort and put flesh on many of the initiatives taken. In this book, I am returning to the past to create a new game for the future.

PART I

Our scholarly ecosystem

2. Where is academia going? Living within a POP culture

"WHERE SHALL I PUBLISH?"

Where is academia going? Universities should support scholarship that addresses the complex questions that matter most to society (Winter, 2011). However, we are experiencing a "publish or perish" (POP) culture, which leads to a requirement for compliance with certain rules of the game that scholars are being told to follow. Research becomes a game, more than an attempt to address questions that matter to society or even to accumulate knowledge. In this book I contribute to changing this game.

I am often asked by students or junior faculty to suggest publication outlets or lists of preferred journals. I find this difficult to respond to as I have signed the San Francisco Declaration (DORA), and thus have committed not to make references to journal impact factors (JIF). However, I tend to respond in three main points. First, publish where you will reach your audience. Second, publish where you will get help in developing an impactful contribution. Impact should have a long-term perspective, and is about research and practice. Third, I see the challenge of the POP culture encountered by most PhD students and junior faculty. They experience great pressure to publish in a specified group of leading journals. In addition, I typically comment that I want to give priority to young and innovative journals, and that the present POP-based incentive regime may have negative consequences for true scholarship and for the future of academia. The POP culture leads to a crisis in research. I have committed to contribute to resolving this crisis.

PUBLISH OR PERISH

What is the "state of the misery"? Under this title, Mats Alvesson made provocations at plenary presentations in 2017 at both the European

Academy of Management (EURAM) and the European Group of Organisation Studies (EGOS) meetings. He claimed that we are seeing more and more management research, but it contributes less and less. "Researchers are becoming less ... scholars, but more ... journal producing technicians. Contemporary academia has become a hothouse for functional stupidity, and the 'success' recipe for individual researchers and departments leads to irrelevant research."[1]

One important part of my academic career has involved taking up invitations from different universities to train their PhD students in getting published. Through exposure to the North American scholarly system at the beginning of the 1990s, I observed the focus on publishing, and I learned how PhD students were trained in how to get their papers published. This knowledge was new to me. It piqued my interest, and I used this experience and these lessons to offer faculty seminars, and PhD courses in how to get published, in Europe. Some of these lessons I still find very valuable, and I still provide some seminars for students on how to publish. However, I also learned about the POP culture, and some of the negative aspects of the publishing game and the associated pressure. In the last part of the 1990s I became more cautious regarding some of the negative consequences of this culture, and I started writing about the "lamp" and "hammer' syndromes involved (Huse, 1996; 1998).

> The ascendancy of neoliberalism and the associated discourses of 'new public management', during the 1980s and 1990s has produced a fundamental shift in the way universities and other institutions of higher education have defined and justified their institutional existence. The traditional professional culture of open intellectual enquiry and debate has been replaced with an institutional stress on performativity, as evidenced by the emergence of an emphasis on measured outputs: on strategic planning, performance indicators, quality assurance measures and academic audits. (Olssen and Peters, 2005: 313)

POP has become a way of life in academia. Its background is in neoliberalism and new public management. Universities and business schools are under attack (Walsh, 2011). Many are afraid that our scholarly integrity and the relevance of our research are questioned. A major challenge to the integrity of management scholarship comes from the escalating competition for publication space in leading journals (Honig and Lampel,

---

[1]   PowerPoint images used by Alvesson at the EGOS and EURAM conferences in 2017.

2018). For our private survival in academia, we are pressed to publish. Writing papers for leading journals is extremely demanding, and may easily take all our scholarly focus.

In a neoliberal culture, universities are being held responsible for where and how much their researchers publish. Academics thus publish whatever they can in print, rather than working on developing serious ideas that may take many years to produce and publish (Moosa, 2018: 173). Denise Shapiro, former president of the Academy of Management (AOM), showed in her outgoing presidential address how this POP culture creates bias (Shapiro, 2017). It creates bias:

- against new and innovative ideas;
- against work from non-English speaking countries;
- against nonarticle publications;
- against teaching and nonpublication research and activities;
- in favor of unscrupulous conference organizers, and the development of predatory, fake, or "black" journals;
- in favor of American publications, including the study of American issues, and the use of American data;
- against the development of local knowledge, and against work on research projects that have a local benefit.

We can easily see that the POP culture has led to an explosion of published research, but unfortunately a deterioration of its quality. Moosa (2018: 173–6) is very critical of this culture: "Academics are pushed to put together whatever they can to get published rather than spending their time and energy on innovative and important ideas that can take years to develop. The relevance to practice becomes lost, and academics write for themselves rather than for practice or policy-making." Moosa is arguing here that the POP culture creates unreliable and biased research findings, including support for underlying hypotheses and against negative findings. POP may lead to HARKing (hypothesizing after results are known), p-hacking, and selective reporting. Moosa also shows that both predatory and nonpredatory journals extract as much money as possible from academics: "There is a ganging-up or team production of publications, including a raise in authorship related misconduct." The POP culture has also been found to be detrimental to the health and wellbeing of the people in our profession.

Shapiro warns that as we as scholars are required to publish, we are not able to spend time on other scholarly activities (Shapiro, 2017).

Universities and business schools come under immense pressure to organize their activities, research centers, and departments to conform as closely as possible to a structure that will maximize their faculties' opportunities to be published in leading journals. One way of monitoring publishing is through journal rankings. Some journals are ranked higher than others, and the ranking systems may vary across nations, universities, and departments. However, in general, in management on a global level, the highest ranked journals are a few US-based ones. There are, for example, no, or at least very few, European-based journals at the top of these ranking lists. Scholars from across the world are thus strongly incentivized to adapt their research efforts to get into these US-based journals.

We are facing a crisis in research (Tourish, 2019). Where is our profession, as scholars, going? Where is our profession, as management scholars, going? Our professional associations, such as the AOM, EURAM, and EGOS, are raising these questions, and senior scholars are severely concerned about it. Mats Alvesson voiced, as mentioned above, concerns at his plenary presentations at the EURAM and EGOS meetings. What is the reality behind Alvesson's provocations? Alvesson, Gabriel, and Paulsen (2017), together with many others, detail these concerns. Alvesson et al, (2017) call for a "return to meaning" and a social science community with something to say. Others are also painting a very critical picture of the present academic publishing game (Hall and Martin, 2019; Moosa, 2018; Tourish, 2019).

Moosa (2018) shows the negative sides of the POP reality that we meet in universities and business schools, and several recent contributions show how this game can lead to professional misconduct (Hall and Martin, 2019; Honig and Lampel, 2018). It is argued that true scholarship and excellence in research are being lost. But what do we mean by true scholarship and excellence in research?

TRUE SCHOLARSHIP

Boyer (1990) made a benchmark contribution to work regarding what true scholarship is. His book has affected present thinking about the role of universities (Hill, 2010) and has been cited by many leading scholars, including several of the AOM presidents in their presidential addresses.

His book reflects that there are several functions which academics are expected to perform. These are:

- Scholarship of discovery (research—what is to be known, what is yet to be found?)
- Scholarship of integration (synthesis—what do the findings mean; how to provide a larger, more comprehensive understanding?)
- Scholarship of application (practice—how can knowledge be helpful to individuals as well as to institutions?)
- Scholarship of teaching (teaching begins with what the teacher knows).

Scholars are academics who conduct research, publish, and then perhaps convey their knowledge to students or apply what they have learned (Boyer, 1990: 15). Boyer argues that the functions of scholarship interact dynamically and form an interdependent whole (1990: 25). He pays particular attention to the loss of reflection in academia.

Boyer observes that 'the dominant view of being a scholar is to be a researcher—and publication is the primary yardstick by which scholars are measured' (Boyer, 1990: 19). However, the scholarship of discovery contributes not only to the stock of human knowledge but also to the intellectual climate of a university. The intellectual climate is about the research process and passion for discovery and integration, not only the outcome. The scholarship of integration involves putting individual research findings into a perspective and context (Boyer, 1990: 19). True scholarship is holistic, interdisciplinary, interpretive, and integrative. Integration gives meaning to isolated facts. This is making research authentic. To be considered scholarship, applications must be tied directly to one's special field of knowledge and relate to this professional activity (1990: 22). If teaching is to be defined as scholarship, it must then both educate and entice future scholars (1990: 23). Teaching as scholarship must stimulate active learning and encourage students to be critical, creative thinkers, with the capacity to go on learning after they have taken their degrees. Good teaching means that faculty, as scholars, are also learners (1990: 24).

Understandings of Boyer's four forms or functions of scholarship have been debated. Boyer's considerations were presented almost 30 years ago in a North American system. It has been claimed that there is now a need for a normative rethinking, for example from Europe (Cern, 2013). Boyer's contribution is still a main benchmark in the evaluation of the POP culture, but in this book I will try to take a closer look at some elements that may help us understand and describe a sustainable culture of true scholarship.

A SUSTAINABLE SCHOLARLY ECOSYSTEM

Do we have a sustainable ecosystem for our profession? An ecosystem is a system that contains a large number of loosely interconnected actors who depend on each other to ensure the overall effectiveness of the system (Baruch, 2013). There are no clear definitions of the elements and contents of a scholarly ecosystem or a research ecosystem. The Responsible Research in Business and Management (RRBM) initiative calls for a change in the research ecosystem and reclaims the need for a scholar identity—that is, the pursuit of knowledge and discovery as well as a focus on impact on both science and policy/practice—over a "getting a paper published" identity (RRBM, 2017). The objective of ecosystem analyses is to create sustainability. An ecosystem will include an analysis of relevant actors, their priorities, and their inter-relationships. Ecosystems will approach equilibriums where one part of the system supports the other parts. However, a change or action in one part will influence the other parts. Thus, an attempt to change one part of an ecosystem may, in order to keep equilibrium, also be defended by the other parts.

I will here set out a scholarly ecosystem that contains five main elements: institutions, audience, message, channels, and community. This ecosystem forms our scholarship and identities, and the challenge is how this ecosystem can contribute to sustainable true scholarship. How can we move from the POP culture to true scholarship? The present equilibrium in the ecosystem is support for the POP culture. Through this book, I will contribute to finding another equilibrium—an equilibrium defined by true scholarship. Figure 2.1 shows this scholarly ecosystem.

The *institutions* element is about our universities or business schools, governments, accreditation, and other agencies that set the standards for evaluating our contribution. *Audience* is who we do research for— ourselves, academia, business, and society. *Message* is what we research on and what we communicate. It is about importance, interest, and innovation. *Channels* are how we disseminate our knowledge and research— through publications, teaching, interventions, and so on. *Community* is about how we as scholars are acting together and about what characterizes our internal interrelationships.

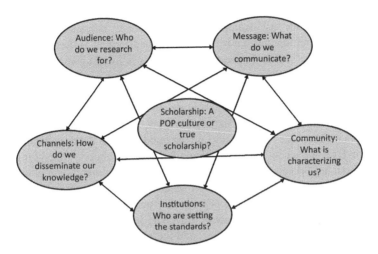

Figure 2.1   The scholarly ecosystem

In the following, I will present the current POP culture status of the various parts of the ecosystem. As in any ecosystem, all parts are strongly interconnected.

Institutions

Where are universities and university scholarships going? Universities and business schools are changing, and they are influenced by a neo-liberal ideology. We are also all influenced by globalization and the digital transformation of society. New needs, methods, and possibilities for financing our institutions are developing. We apply new methods of attracting students, and international student mobility is increasing. Blended learning and new ways of teaching are developed and considered. New standards for and ways of evaluating research, academics, and universities are facilitated, including the use of bibliometrics. Furthermore, we are experiencing new needs in business and society that must be addressed. These changes have impacts on the scholarly ecosystem, including the way in which our institutions are working and being organized, and again on our scholarships. Several authors claim that our institutions are negatively affecting scholarships (Adler and Harzing, 2009).

In their classic contributions, Mintzberg (1979) and Etzioni (1959) used universities as examples of professional bureaucracies. The prime coordination mechanism in such organizations is, according to Mintzberg, the standardization of skills. This is in contrast to machine bureaucracies or divisionalized forms, where the main coordination mechanism is the standardization of work processes or output, respectively. The operating core, which is the faculty, is the key part of the organization in the professional organization, while it is the technostructure in the machine bureaucracy and the middle line in the divisionalized form. Universities today, and particularly business schools, are no longer professional bureaucracies. They are becoming machine bureaucracies. Standardization of work processes and output has become the key coordination mechanism; the professional training and socialization of faculty has a decreasing impact in university life. The technostructure is increasing in size and importance, and the roles of middle management administrators as department heads are becoming more formalized.

Academics have typically been recruited to universities and business schools because of scholarly identities and intrinsic motivation of scholarship. For many this has been like a religious calling. We have, however, recently seen a specialization in academic positions. Moosa (2018: 173) argues that in a POP culture, the people who progress will be those that find a place in the bureaucracy. Academics wanting to avoid publication pressure are typically those filling these middle management positions (Moosa, 2018: 173).

Universities are increasingly being scrutinized by accreditation agencies, which pressurize them both to perform and to adhere to global standardization. However, universities, scholarly traditions, and research vary across cultures and continents, and even across countries. The European Foundation for Management Development (EFMD) acknowledges through its EQUIS accreditations that there is a key difference between European and US schools (Wilson and McKiernan, 2011). Research output from European universities and business schools may be difficult or inappropriate to place in the top US-based journals. Accreditations may, however, serve to uphold a North American elite, thereby defining what is considered a "good" business school:

> For example, EQUIS usually recommends future changes for schools it accredits in an attempt to nurture development and innovation. Normative pressures are placed on organizations from the state and other regulatory bodies. Conformity to these pressures results in organizations changing their

structures and processes to become aligned with these institutionally pre-
scribed expectations. (Wilson and McKiernan, 2011: 460)

Thus accreditations force important choices in business schools.

Rankings of business schools and universities are not new, but globalization and standardization have contributed to a stronger focus on
such rankings. Rankings may be important for both external and internal
stakeholders. They may be important for employee loyalty and identity,
but also for the economic future of the universities and business schools
(Kogut, 2008). Rankings may be used internally as a mechanism by which
to judge the institution's own quality. However, rankings are not simply
mechanical, objective measures. The development of digitalization has
increased possibilities of using various types of bibliometric analyses for
rankings, and standards and experiences from North America have been
influential in how to define quality. Institutions worldwide now exert
pressure on their faculty to publish in predefined "top" journals. This has
the effect of reinforcing the prestige and ranking of the journals.

There are many problems with journal rankings. Defining which journals are the prestigious, top-rated ones is also difficult, since different
lists of rankings include different journals. However, journal rankings are
being used by universities and business schools to evaluate their faculty,
including in terms of recruitment and giving tenure. The rankings are
largely based on isomorphism and definitions from granting agencies.

International management research has increasingly been influenced
by North American research standards. There is a trend to use a US-based
yardstick to assess research quality (Starkey and Madan, 2001). This is
reflected in the tendency to view publication in leading US management
journals as synonymous with research excellence. However, Starkey and
Madan argue that American academics themselves are questioning their
own research norms (2001: s8).

Universities and institutions must not forget that their real power
comes from great ideas and the people that are creating them, and that
their role should be to support scholarship that addresses the complex
questions that matter most to society. Adler and Harzing (2009) question
whether the academic ranking systems that are being used to rank scholars, universities, and journals undermine rather than foster and reward
scholarship that matters. Rather than allowing assessments and ranking
systems to continue to consume disproportionate amounts of universities'
attention and resources, academia needs to shift to designing and implementing environments that purposefully encourage research that matters.

Audience

Who do we do research for? Who are our end users and with whom do we want to have a dialogue? Research has traditionally been directed by pay makers—whether this is the Church or the state.

Management research is often criticized for not meeting the needs of practitioners, either in business or in policy making. Management research is often not respected outside academia. However, even within academia it is criticized (Alvesson and Gabriel, 2013: 252). Its audience is usually only a narrow group within the academy. The audience for many journal submissions is not a community of scholars, but a small community of likely reviewers. It is the publication itself that is important. Silencing reviewers' criticism may be more important than communicating something meaningful or socially useful. The audience of our research includes journals and journal editors.

The audience of our research is those that are evaluating us, and most often that is the institutions, including departments and those setting the evaluation standards, which are being evaluated by accreditation agencies and funders at different levels. The audience will be those that are evaluating our present and future positions.

Publishing has become a means in itself. The publication process is supposed to be a way of controlling the quality of research, but most often it is not a way to reach an audience with a message. In a POP culture, we are typically writing for ourselves. Rewarding scholars for publishing may lead to misconduct and the breaking of scholarly norms (Davis, 2015). The design of the publishing system itself promotes misconduct: we are writing because of pressure and/or positive incentives. The purpose is often that of meeting various ranking criteria set up by various pay makers. However, the content of our research and publishing might not be the most important thing.

In the discussion of audience, we face several existential questions for our scholarly future. Are we reflecting on the various sets of stakeholders as our end users? Do we consider the future of our society as an end user and audience? How do we include the audience in the development of our research?

Message

What do we communicate? "The present incentive system does not care about what is published, whether it is fraudulent or useless" (Moosa,

2018: 172). I repeatedly tell my students that their work should be "important, innovative and interesting." That is what I learned from my research methods classes during the 1970s. However, this is not always what is being communicated today. Warnings are therefore now voiced that management research lacks relevance and impact. The message of our research and publications is often too incremental and narrow; the approach is too much about gap spotting and overly guided by holes in existing research. When searching for gaps in the literature we typically find topics and approaches that are unimportant or uninteresting. There is a gap-spotting incrementalism in the present POP culture.

What is relevance? Do we address the grand challenges of the world (McGahan, 2018)? Management research is criticized as not relevant to the world around us (Rousseau, 2006). RRBM calls for actions to transform business and management research toward achieving a better world. It introduces principles about the usefulness and credibility of knowledge to guide research. RRBM has a vision that business schools worldwide should be admired for their contribution to societal wellbeing (Tsui, 2018).

This follows the arguments also presented by Alvesson et al. (2017), Alvesson and Sandberg (2013), and Boyer (1990). RRBM argues for a system that goes beyond theoretical gap spotting, and that management scholars, including doctoral students, should be trained to speak to practitioners. We should "not foster a gap-spotting mode, but a scholarship mode" (Alvesson and Sandberg, 2013: 137). Alvesson and Gabriel (2013) attack the gap-spotting formulaic conformity of our research. Formulaic research involves extreme specialization, an incremental and excessively cautious attitude towards theoretical contributions, formulaic methodologies, and a standardized article presentation targeted at very narrow and sympathetic academic communities (Alvesson and Gabriel, 2013: 245). Even AOM President Carol Kulik warned, in her presidential address in 2019, that academics rarely interface with end users.

The POP culture has forced academics to downgrade their primary aim from making discoveries to publishing as many papers as possible—in highly ranked leading journals.

The channels

How do we communicate with end users? How do we disseminate our knowledge and research? Are publications in leading journals the best way of disseminating our work? Moosa disagrees: "The vast majority of work published in academic journals these days does not meet the objective of accumulation of knowledge and disseminating it to a wider community" (Moosa, 2018: 173).

Publication in scientific journals, and particularly in some leading journals, seems to be a goal in itself. I disagree with that, and I see journal publication as one of several channels for our messages to reach our audiences with the purpose of achieving an objective. Journal publication is thus only a mean to reach an objective. Scientific journal publications may be one good way of communication, but not necessarily the best one. Some additional elements need to be considered. Which journals and which types of publication are the best channels for reaching our objectives? Does the pressure to publish in highly ranked leading journals hinder us in reaching our audience? Are there other ways we should disseminate our research and knowledge—in addition to or instead of publications? Publications in leading journals may be the best choice if this is the objective in itself, and we are incentivized or pressed to this in the POP culture. However, other channels should be considered if the objective is to contribute to the wellbeing of others and to create a better world (Shapiro, 2017; Tsui, 2013). Our responsibility is not to ourselves (Hambrick, 1994). What about teaching, speeches, consulting, and mentoring? The pressure to publish in leading journals is creating flaws in the dissemination processes.

The discussion of communication channels focuses on journals, but only on premiere journals. Warnings, for example by Alvesson, are raised that in this way we are creating publishing technicians rather than true scholars. One line of discussion is that of metrics and academic ranking: how this system is leading to scientific misconduct (Honig et al., 2017). Moosa (2018) focuses on the negative consequences of the POP situation in the academic system. He argues that POP is a symptom of a neoliberal market ideology. In several contributions, Adler and Harzing (for example, Adler and Harzing, 2009) have shown the problems in the present, dominant journal impact factor (JIF) ranking system, and Honig et al. (2017) show how scientific misconduct can follow. Furthermore, Hall and Martin (2019) present a taxonomy of research misconduct in management research. Such misconduct can be found in most disciplines, but business schools are particularly vulnerable to them (Hall and Martin, 2019). Problems with misconduct in business schools may be more frequent, as consequence control is usually lower here than elsewhere, businesses rarely being directly harmed by the research conducted in business schools.

The arbitrariness of journal rankings has received considerable attention. Starbuck (2005), for example, argues that it makes no sense to judge articles solely on the journal in which they appear. Lower prestige journals also publish excellent articles and high prestige journals publish pedestrian articles.

Most top ranked management journals are North American-based. These journals usually describe themselves as international. However, this can be questioned. Adler and Harzing (2009) show that their editorial boards are almost exclusively national; their authorship is predominantly US-based; and even where the international spread of authorship is expanding, this can be camouflaged by US academics working outside the US or by the inclusion of US-based coauthors. Even where the international spread of authorship is expanding, it still mostly involved US-based academics working outside the US, US-trained scholars, or US-based coauthors.

Finally, language should also be mentioned. Academic reflections and research have developed over history in many countries and in many languages. There may be streams of research that are the building blocks of various national contributions but may, because of language, not be used in English language journals. That may also be the case for more recent contributions. Contributions in languages other than English exist, but are not often searched for in the present system. Furthermore, a language is often a reflection of a culture and the particular situation in a culture. Even if there are possibilities of translation from one language to another, it may be difficult to translate the deeper aspects of culture and cultural challenges.

Community

Do we as a community believe in the significance of advanced thinking and research in management (Hambrick, 1994)? I have my identity in my scholarly values, and my scholarship is sacred for me. However, there are pressures facing our scholarly values. Walsh (2011) claims that the relentless ratings and rankings of our work have stolen the sacredness of our scholarship. As noted previously, Alvesson, in his various keynote speeches and publications, warns that we in the POP culture are moving from scholars to publishing technicians.

It can be argued that global scholarship is defined within the West, and in particular North America (Alsbach et al., 2004). This globalization may lead to "a McDonaldism of universities" and a concomitant

McDonaldized evaluation of us as scholars. This standardization may go beyond globalization, to also have consequences across faculty and across experiences.

In our community we need to appreciate experience, not only evaluations based on McDonaldism. In the POP culture, expectations of senior scholars will be similar to those of junior faculty and PhD students. We are all being evaluated based on the same standards—how we make our hamburgers and how fast we are able to serve our customers. We are all being evaluated based on our regularity of publication in leading journals. This may result in 30 single years of experience being given priority over 30 years of accumulated experience. Scholars being raised in the system fight for the system because that is what they know and where they have created their careers. Therefore, I return in Chapter 3 to the experiences and reflections of previous AOM presidents, such as, for example, Duane Ireland and David Whetten.

> Our scholarship typically varies across the seasons of our careers. As we know, at the beginning of our careers, we typically concentrate on the scholarship of discovery and integration. In the middle part of our careers, and perhaps almost certainly towards their end—based on a wealth of experience—many of us choose to increase our efforts in terms of application. (Ireland, 2015: 153)

The scholarship community is a fellowship among colleagues. Senior scholars should use their voices to support and mentor their younger colleagues. The community is supported by sharing, open, honest, and trusting relationships (Whetten, 2001). Individual credit and the protection of individual research projects and findings are becoming standard. We are losing our sense of community.

A final warning relates to the challenges of legal and ethical misconduct. The POP culture may easily stimulate fabrication, falsification, and plagiarism, as well as various questionable research practices (Hall and Martin, 2019; Honig and Lampel, 2018).

EXISTING STATUS IN THE POP CULTURE

In this chapter, I have described the academic POP culture and compared it with true scholarship. Ideally, we would like to see true scholarship, but the POP culture is embedded in an ecosystem equilibrium that resists individual initiatives for change. Those that benefit the most from the system will hardly be those that will champion the changes (Özbilgin,

2009). I thus urge those with influence to go beyond the standards that benefit the most from the present POP culture ecosystem equilibrium. I have here described the various parts of this scholarly ecosystem.

Our current ecosystem is reinforcing research that is narrow, outdated, often destructive, and insulated from the real world. We should contribute to encouraging and supporting efforts to change the POP culture-based ecosystem to one that supports the principles associated with true scholarship and that contributes to a better world. Here is a brief summary of this chapter's findings:

- Institutions are formed by a neoliberal market ideology with external incentives, and authority is exercised through a top-down approach.
- The audience is typically a narrow group in academia, and our work is rarely respected outside academia.
- The message is incremental, it is gap-spotting and seeking holes in existing literature; it is standardized, work in progress is being hidden; the focus is usually short term, and based on the past.
- The channel is journals, but only premiere journals. This is tenure track-driven and results in the "hammer" and "lamp" syndromes.
- It is a community in which the winner takes it all; it is based on self-reliance, and we become less scholars and more journal producing technicians.

My objective through the rest of the book is to contribute to an equilibrium which helps to sustain true scholarship.

3. AOM presidential speeches 1993–2018[1]

ACADEMY OF MANAGEMENT AND WHAT MATTERS MOST

Introduction to the AOM

The Academy of Management (AOM) was established in 1936.[2] In 2019 it had about 20,000 members from nearly 120 nations, and it had 25 different divisions or interest groups. The present vision of AOM is to inspire and enable a better world through its scholarship and teaching about management and organizations. The AOM mission is to build a vibrant and supportive community of scholars by markedly expanding opportunities to connect and explore ideas. Several of the leading scientific journals in management are owned by the AOM, including the "top ranked" journals *Academy of Management Journal* (AMJ) and *Academy of Management Review* (AMR). The annual conference in 2019 had more than 11,000 participants.

The first time I attended the AOM meeting was in Atlanta in 1993. It was then called the "national academy" in contrast to the "regional academies." There were about 3,000 participants at the Atlanta meeting, and very few were from outside North America. For this meeting I had papers accepted and presented in three different divisions.

I had got to know Carolyn Dexter from involvement in other associations. At the AOM meeting in 1993 she invited me to join the AOM International Programs Committee (IPC) that she was about to form. Its

---

[1] As I was preparing this book, and this chapter in particular, I used the same material to write a chapter in a book that was a retirement tribute to Professor Torger Reve (Huse, 2019).
[2] The figures here about AOM build on information from the AOM website: https://aom.org/About-AOM/History.aspx accessed September 17, 2019.

charge was to contribute to the internationalization of AOM. This charge had two parts: first, to increase the participation of non-US scholars; second, to increase the international awareness of the AOM members. The mandate of the committee was given by the AOM board of governors, and in particular Richard Mowday, the program chair elect at the 1993 AOM meeting. The members of the committee were partly from the International Management Division and partly came from or had affiliations outside the US. During the 1993 meeting, the IPC arranged a Saturday night open event and a Sunday lunch committee meeting. This was the starting point for my ten years of intensive involvement in the IPC (from 2001 reorganized and followed by the International Themes Committee). I was the IPC director in the period 1998–2001. During these ten years, I had close relationships with the AOM presidents and its board of governors. In the years 2000 and 2001, I was also nominated as a candidate for its board of governors, but was not elected.

At the 1993 AOM annual conference, the annual presidential lunch was arranged for a Tuesday, and at the end of the lunch the outgoing president, Donald Hambrick, gave a speech reflecting on his experiences as AOM president. His speech was published the following year in AMR, and the title of his address was "What if the Academy really mattered?" The address was a challenge to us as scholars and members of AOM. Hambrick argued that our responsibility as scholars was not to ourselves, but rather to the institutions and individuals around the world that are in direct need of improved management. "It is time for us to matter." In order to increase the international-mindedness of the AOM membership, he also suggested that AOM should at some point in the future hold its annual meeting outside North America. He also stated that from 1994 onward, AOM would appoint its own professional administration.

Thirteen former AOM presidents participated in a panel at the AOM annual conference in Chicago in August 2018. They spoke about what matters most for us as scholars, discussed the state of the art, and presented their concerns for the future. The background was a Responsible Research in Business and Management (RRBM) initiative. They shared concerns about the use of metrics and the relevance of published research.

Presidential Addresses—What Matters Most?

The presidents of AOM all give a reflective presidential address at the end of their presidential period. It usually contains reflections and recommendations from the outgoing presidents about what matters most for the development of the profession as management scholars. They typically address what they see as the most important issues or challenges for the AOM, for management research, and for scholarship in general. The addresses are published in the AMR. The addresses are thus easy to access. Table 3.1 contains an overview of key points from AOM Presidential Addresses from 1993 to 2018. I have thus analyzed the addresses of 25 former AOM presidents. The table contains the year of the presentation and not the year of publication in AMR. In the table, I have extracted what I see as key sentences from my analyses of the addresses.

REFLECTIONS FROM OUTGOING AOM PRESIDENTS

Below I present citations of the outgoing AOM presidents' arguments and reflections.[3] They are sorted into eight points that I found were addressed by many of the presidents. The eight issues presented are: scholarly identity, dysfunctional metrics, lack of relevance, role of institutions, reframing international dialogues, creating a sustainable community, importance of compassion, and research for the future.

---

[3]   The citations in this section are based on the presentations at the meetings, and thus there may be minor deviations from the *AMR* published papers. My analysis took place in several steps, and I read each presidential address several times. In the first round of analysis, I sorted into groups and subgroups the issues of concern raised by the various presidents. This sorting resulted in the list of eight main concerns presented below. In the second round, the various concerns were distributed in a matrix across the various presidents. The lack of relevance was the concern raised by most presidents, followed by dysfunctional metrics and creating a sustainable community. Lee's address is an example of how many of the concerns were integrated. Finally, I sorted the concerns and arguments from the presidents according to the previously presented scholarly ecosystem framework. Huse (2019) offers an analysis of the presidential addresses, and this chapter is building on and using that article. For validation reasons, a version of Huse (2019) was sent to the past presidents for comment. I received important responses from several of them, and overall, more than half responded. Their responses are incorporated into this book. Their feedback was highly appreciated.

Table 3.1   *Outgoing presidents' reflections*

Address year	TITLE AMR ARTICLE (publication the year after address held) Core messages/citations
1993 *Hambrick*	WHAT IF THE ACADEMY ACTUALLY MATTERED? Our responsibility is not to ourselves – If we believe in the significance of advanced thinking and research on management, then it is time we showed it. (1994: 13) – To a great extent, the role of a scholar is in the middle category: to observe, analyze, critique, and disseminate. (1994: 16)
1994 *Oldham*	Address not published
1995 *Von Glinow*	ON MINORITY RIGHTS AND MAJORITY ACCOMMODATIONS Few people seem to take responsibility for their actions – As a society of professionals, whose very essence is based on debate and the pursuit and dissemination of knowledge, we can ill afford to succumb to politically correct method acting for fear of stepping out of line. (1996: 350)
1996 *Mowday*	REAFFIRMING OUR SCHOLARLY VALUES Place scholarship and scholarly values at the center – challenges and pressures for change faced by business schools are great. What are the implications for our scholarly values? On the one hand, we can view the pressures as a threat to our scholarly values. On the other hand, the challenges we face might be viewed as a golden opportunity to reaffirm our scholarly values. (1997: 338) – our definition of scholarship has narrowed over time. For many, scholarship has come to represent publishing research in refereed journals rather than the broader search for and dissemination and application of new knowledge. (1997: 338)
1997 *Hitt*	TWENTY-FIRST CENTURY ORGANIZATIONS: BUSINESS FIRMS, BUSINESS SCHOOLS, AND THE ACADEMY Eliminate the US-phobic approach to management education and research – Please notice that I do not suggest "control," "govern," or "oversee," but, rather, we should work with our colleagues [*international affiliate associations*] as partners. By helping them develop these organizations, we all will benefit. Frankly, if we do not take actions like these, such organizations are likely to develop independently, leaving the Academy the opportunity at some point in the future of becoming much less relevant or, possibly, even an irrelevant organization. The Academy needs bold actions in the global arena now. (1998: 222) – We must also continue the process created several years ago of ensuring that this research reaches executives through the popular business press. They need our help, and we need their support. Thus, we should pursue cooperative strategies; alliances with executives/managers and deans can and should be mutually beneficial. (1998: 224)

Address year	TITLE AMR ARTICLE (publication the year after address held) Core messages/citations
1998 *Starbuck*	OUR SHRINKING EARTH What we see depends strongly on what we want or expect to see – The scholars in different nations evolve semi-independent intellectual traditions. For instance, population ecology is popular in the United States, structuration in Britain, postmodern deconstruction in France, and longitudinal case studies in Scandinavia. These differences often nurture claims of superiority and allegations of irrelevance. In my experience, however, the existence of sharply contrasting views has always turned out to be a sign that neither side is wrong and that both sides have validity. We gain more, I think, if we regard each intellectual tradition as having value to contribute and as deserving of respect. (1999: 190)
1999 *Huff*	CHANGES IN ORGANIZATIONAL KNOWLEDGE PRODUCTION We need to consider new strategic positions closer to the knowledge production within the organizations we study – I have in mind something that my colleagues in England call a "virtuous circle." The issues of importance to Mode 1.5 typically will rise from practice and will be defined in conversation with those in practice, but other insights should be solicited and integrated. The relevant data will come primarily, but not entirely, from practice. (2000: 292)
2000 *Whetten*	WHAT MATTERS MOST Always aspiring to be better, human beings. To share with one another what truly matters most – These terms *[together and a fellowship]* suggest that the business of academe is best accomplished when it is encompassed within a social fabric characterized by open, honest, and trusting relationships. (2001: 176) – each of us can contribute to building, from the bottom up, an academic professional association that reflects the truest expression of collegium-a fellowship among colleagues. (2001: 177)
2001 *Van de Ven*	THIS ACADEMY IS FOR YOU! The Academy is committed to shaping the future of management research and education. – We have the opportunity to pass it on by building a better infrastructure for the next generation of management scholars. We all play a role—as researchers, teachers, consultants, managers, and students—and we all make what the Academy is to us. Through all the energy, fuss, and worry that you and I contribute to the Academy, we are realizing our ambitions of becoming a part of something bigger than we can ever accomplish individually. (2002: 171) – We do not seek to be a global academy of management and colonize the world. Rather, we seek to enlighten ourselves about our global profession and to confederate with associations throughout the world to accomplish this. There is so much we should share with and can learn from each other. (2002: 175) – Provide a supportive and dynamic community for learning and sharing. (2001: 182)

Address year	TITLE AMR ARTICLE (publication the year after address held)
	Core messages/citations
2002	A DREAM FOR THE ACADEMY
Bartunek	To make a positive difference in the world for the profession of management, the advancement of which is our primary mission
	– But I believe that being nurturing and developmental actually is at least a part of how we are with all of these when we are at our best. (2003: 201)
	– How much life and vitality does your work bring to you and to others? (2003: 203)
2003	WHAT DO WE KNOW AND HOW DO WE REALLY KNOW IT?
Pearce	Build on the intellectual work of others and conduct research in which we seek to carefully check claims
	– I want to be a reflective observer who uses my time doing some real, serious organizational management to learn more about what we know as scholars and how we know it. (2004: 175)
	– I believe that both worlds would be enriched if the overlap were just a little bit bigger. More folk wisdom could be subjected to careful analysis and the more systematic reality checks that could improve its veracity. And the powerful tools of scholarship could be harnessed for truly important organizational problems. (2004: 178)
2004	REFLECTIONS ON ENGENDERING A SUSTAINABLE COMMUNITY
Tung	WITHIN THE ACADEMY
	Balancing educating the mind with educating the heart
	– Others disagreed, asserting that although our journals appear to be receptive to different topics, they publish only those articles that conform to "North American research templates." To put it differently, it appears that while authors from around the world can meet with success in getting their research published, this is only as long as they have been socialized into the North American "way of thinking and methodology." (2005: 240)
	– This apparent loss of a sense of community may sometimes lead us to undertake actions and to engage in behavior that might be perceived as selfish, self-centered, and sometimes even downright hurtful. To put it differently, have we, in the course of our single-minded pursuit of generating new knowledge—that is, educating the mind—ignored the need to educate the heart? (2005: 243)
2005	EVIDENCE-BASED MANAGEMENT
Rousseau	Evidence-based management means translating principles based on best evidence into organizational practices
	– Evidence-based management, in my opinion, provides the needed model to guide the closing of the research–practice gap. (2006: 260)

Address year	TITLE AMR ARTICLE (publication the year after address held)
	Core messages/citations
2006	QUEST FOR AN ENGAGED ACADEMY
Cummings	It is our duty and responsibility to make sure that our knowledge makes the world a better place.
	– Forging closer links between research and practice is a key part of our mission and values, and unless we become much better at it, we risk being seen as moral hypocrites. (2007: 357)
	– Engaged research might help us identify important variables and explanations not previously considered, discover entirely new organizational forms and practices, or tap into the tacit knowledge that underlies so much practice. It might even help us make the world a better place. (2007: 358)
	– it is our duty and responsibility to make sure that our knowledge makes the world a better place. (2007: 359)
2007	FIGHTING THE ORTHODOXY: LEARNING TO BE PRAGMATIC
Smith	Let's be passionate about our ideas but creative and somewhat pragmatic in presenting them to the market
	– Right between scholars trying to get their ideas accepted and gatekeepers making judgments on their scholarship stands the painful truth that what constitutes a contribution or adequate contribution can be determined only over time. And here is another painful truth: it is not always easy to judge what contributions will prove to be the piece of knowledge we need to move our field forward, as we can see from Jay Barney's experience in publishing his influential paper on firm resources. (2008: 307)
	– Let's keep high standards for scholarship, encouraging passionate scholars to do their best work while maintaining an open mind about their unique contributions. Let's demonstrate more perspective, compassion, and empathy. (2008: 307)
2008	THE MANAGEMENT PROFESSOR
Lee	Scholarly contributions should be evaluated by the subsequent knowledge they inspire
	– When I think about our academic research, it's been my experience that one publication seldom has a large influence on our theory and research. Instead, it is a stream of programmatic research involving many different kinds of books, articles, and chapters that deeply affects our thinking and actions. (2009: 197)
	– First, we should be *less* concerned about the contribution of individual studies and *more* concerned about the contribution of programmatic bodies of research. Further, I believe that such programmatic research should be our gold standard for meaningful academic scholarship. Second, most contemporary research issues and the everyday constraints imposed by a business school require a diverse skill set and multiple points of view for programmatic scholarship, particularly in today's global marketplace for research and publication. In other words, I believe that team-based research is the most effective strategy to conduct programmatic scholarship in today's environment. (2009: 197–8)

Address year	TITLE AMR ARTICLE (publication the year after address held) Core messages/citations
2009 *DeNisi*	CHALLENGES AND OPPORTUNITIES FOR THE ACADEMY IN THE NEXT DECADE Better job of connecting our research to the world around us – We need to decide what the nature of the relationship will be between the Academy and its affiliates … Early discussions in the strategic planning sessions seemed to point to a desire, on our part, to be leaders in a global consortium. Of course, that assumes that others would want us as leaders, or even as participants in such an effort. (2010: 192) – We really need to look at research programs and streams rather than individual studies. … therefore, perhaps we should be encouraging young scholars to develop coherent research programs, rather than rewarding them for publishing the "five required A-level articles" necessary for tenure (2010:195)
2010 *Walsh*	EMBRACING THE SACRED IN OUR SECULAR SCHOLARLY WORLD The relentless rating and ranking of our work and even journal lists and rankings have stolen the sacredness of our scholarship – Something is keeping us from being all that we can be … In so doing, I will talk about the audit culture that has emerged around us, our problematic reaction to it, and the consequences of that reaction. (2011: 215) – The problem is that we have reproduced and internalized this audit culture in our own universities. I fear for our future if that culture is left unchecked. (2011: 217) – I began my remarks by saying that we live in an audit culture, one born of a deep interest in what we do. Society cares deeply about how we actually inspire and enable a better world. The problem is that society does not know exactly how to appraise our work. All of those rating and ranking schemes reflect earnest attempts to make sense of what we do, but they do not really know what they are looking for. (2011: 229)
2011 *Jackson*	We @aom – address not published
2012 *Tsui*	ON COMPASSION IN SCHOLARSHIP: WHY SHOULD WE CARE? When we are judged only on how many papers we publish … we lose meaning in our work. – The research I did in preparing this address convinced me that daring to care is crucial for our world. Compassion is essential for a sustainable future, both socially and environmentally. (2013: 167) – "Some people have come to believe that business schools are harmful to society, fostering self-interested, unethical and even illegal behavior among their graduates" … Many forces have caused this condition, but high on the list is the "publish or perish" environment that all scholars face. This publication pressure parallels the focus on a few of the (mostly American) top-tier journals. (2013: 175)

Address year	TITLE AMR ARTICLE (publication the year after address held)
	Core messages/citations
2012 Tsui (continued)	– The discussion seems to conclude that the Academy is filled with heartless researchers and teachers who focus only on advancing their self-interested goal of promotion and tenure. (2013: 176) – Change requires concerted efforts from all of us. I call for all Academy members to join the board in leading the change, each in his or her own way. This is the power of the collective. Together, we can make a huge difference in changing the state of our profession for the better. I invite all to accept the compassion pledge by summoning the courage to conduct research that inspires managers to lead compassionately, to teach in ways that lead our students to act justly, to help our young colleagues make a difference, and to serve in ways that lead to a better Academy and a better world. (2013: 177)
2013 Chen	BECOMING AMBICULTURAL: A PERSONAL QUEST, AND ASPIRATION FOR ORGANIZATIONS What exactly it means to be a "scholar" and how a scholar should engage with others and with the professional community and society at large – "Be yourself, and aspire steadfastly to the highest levels of integrity and dignity." (2014: 121) – In accord with this ancient tradition, Chinese intellectuals, in fact, are not considered scholars until they "practice what they preach." (2014: 125) – Ambiculturalism offers a framework for valuing other cultures and traditions. But it can only emerge if we have a thorough understanding of our own "culture"—our assumptions, values, foundational ethics, strengths, and shortcomings. Absent this, we can neither fully comprehend nor value other cultures. (2014: 132)
2014 Ireland	OUR ACADEMY, OUR FUTURE A scholar as a learned person who is committed to taking the actions required to fully understand a discipline – Moreover, our focus on scholarship typically varies across the seasons of our careers. As we know, at the beginning of our careers, we typically concentrate on the scholarships of discovery and integration. In the middle part of our careers, and perhaps almost certainly toward their end—based on a wealth of experience— many of us choose to increase our efforts in terms of the scholarship of application. (2015: 153) – collegial community that enables us to inspire, nurture, and support each other as we grow as scholars and create value for those we serve? (2015: 158) – Bringing scholars together from across the world to collaboratively create knowledge, bring perspective to isolated and disparate facts, creatively apply knowledge in impactful ways, and actively disseminate knowledge to others (2015: 160)

Address year	TITLE AMR ARTICLE (publication the year after address held)
	Core messages/citations
2015	OUR TEACHING MISSION
Adler	Our role as educators—how can we respond to the changing societal and institutional context?
	– Alongside the traditional business disciplines, students will need a better understanding of history, politics, sociology, and economics. They will need stronger research skills and greater facility with a broader range of data types … More fundamentally, perhaps, our students will need deeper critical thinking skills. As I just argued, it is not obvious how firms can or should respond to these sustainable development challenges, (2016: 188)
	– giving greater weight to critical thinking, negotiation, environmental and cultural sensitivity, and so forth. This also calls for new action skills, since leadership in this new context will be far more distributed and virtues like courage more critical. (2016: 189)
	– it is urgent, I believe, that, as scholars and educators, we take the initiative, rather than reacting defensively. We need to work with colleagues in other business school departments and elsewhere in the university to articulate a more viable vision of the role of the university (2015: 190)
2016	MAKING THE ACADEMY FULL-VOICE MEANINGFUL
Shapiro	The pressure to publish in A journals affects the lives of management scholars at all career phase
	– Whether you agree or not with this entire list, one thing is certain: the pressure to publish in only A journals affects what scholars write, what scholars cite in their papers, what outlets scholars seek for their papers, what scholars teach, what service scholars provide, and what types of research studies scholars design. As a result, the pressure to publish in A journals affects not only the lives of scholars seeking tenured faculty positions but also the lives of management scholars at all career phases. (2017: 170)
	– This trend of scholarly voice restriction, if uncorrected, risks robbing meaningfulness from not only our Academy but also the progression of management science, the advancement of which depends on the extent to which scholars are encouraged and, hence, willing to share their views, cite other scholars' views, and, thus, ultimately learn from engaged scholarship. (2017:173)

| Address year | TITLE AMR ARTICLE (publication the year after address held) |
	Core messages/citations
2017	FREEDOM IN SCHOLARSHIP: LESSONS FROM ATLANTA
McGahan	Grasp the implications of the problems around us, and use our multidisciplinary perspectives, collegiality, and engagement with practice to do work now that, in the future, we can look back on with real satisfaction, knowing that we improved the lives of everyone around us.
	– First, I invite you to free yourself to work only on things that are both important in the world and have meaning for you personally. Say no to everything else. Be ambitious; address problems deeply and comprehensively in broad research programs. Make each paper and teaching assignment a piece of a bigger puzzle on how organizations can meaningfully improve lives. This means that we have to expand our thinking about data and methods and theory. (2018: 175)
	– Make sure that, at the end of your career, you can look back with satisfaction that you've stood against suffering, inequality, and impoverishment; that you've stood for freedom, sustainability, and creativity; that you've used the prosperity you enjoy to make the world better. (2018: 175)
	– We need to support scholars who are dealing with important, difficult, intractable problems, even if the theory is imperfect, the data are incomplete, and the methods are messy. Cultivating an understanding in print of enfranchisement and prosperity will require an investment by all of us in developing new theory, methods, and empirics. We will have to do this together as researchers and as adjudicators of research. (2018: 175–6)
	– The opportunity before us is to grasp the implications of the problems around us at the beginning of the twenty-first century, and to use our multidisciplinary perspectives, collegiality, and engagement with practice to do work now that, in the future, we can look back on with real satisfaction, knowing that we improved the lives of everyone around us. (2018: 178)
2018	THE MISSION OF COMMUNITY
Glynn	Our responsibility is to the world we live in—not only to ourselves
	– WHAT IF ... we recognized that, as a scholarly community, our responsibilities are not only to ourselves but to the world we live in?
	– WHAT IF ... we stood together collectively, as a scholarly community, and used our knowledge and research to advance the institutions around the world in need of help?
	– WHAT IF ... we become, as a scholarly community, more outward looking, to the audiences beyond those of the Academy, to take action to better society and improve lives? (2019)

The Role of Scholars and Scholarly Identity

The theme being the most repeated was about the role of scholars and scholarly identity. They addressed the crisis in research and called for ways of resolving it. This was a core concern already in the addresses from Hambrick, von Glinow, and Mowday in the early and mid 1990s, but was also a main theme in the addresses of later presidents, for example Van de Ven, Tsui, Chen, Ireland, Adler, and Shapiro. Boyer's 1990 book was a main point of reference in concerns regarding the role of scholars.

The role of a scholar is to observe, analyze, critique, and disseminate. (Hambrick)

An inclusive view of what it means to be a scholar is needed. (Mowday)

We need to create value for others and use a broad scope of scholarship, including discovery, integration, application, and teaching. (Ireland)

We must place scholarship and scholarly values at the center of what we as faculty members are being asked to contribute to. (Mowday)

We should be precise about exactly it means to be a "scholar" and how a scholar should engage with others and with the professional community and society at large. (Chen)

A scholar is a learned person who is committed to taking the actions required to fully understand a discipline. (Ireland)

In his 2013 address, Chen included perspectives from China and Chinese wisdom. He suggested that this wisdom is important for understanding scholarly values. The Chinese perspectives include:

Integrity (expectations of both Chinese and Western societies and both academic and business communities), harmony (sharing, mutual respect, reciprocity, and enduring relationships as essential for maintaining a nurturing and supportive community), balance (between the Chinese and Western worlds, between scholarship and practice, and between career and life), integration (bridge the gap between Chinese and Western cultures and practices), dynamics (evolving nature of our community and the changing needs and expectations of our members as they advance in their careers), and independence (concentrate on serving our community members, to hear what they want, and to understand how best to serve them). (Chen)

Adler emphasized the teaching mission of being a scholar. Ireland also addressed how Boyer's types of scholarship could vary over time.

> Some of us focus on only one or two types of scholarship at a point in time, whereas others of us may seek to balance our contributions across all four. Moreover, our focus on scholarship typically varies across the seasons of our careers. (Ireland)

Dysfunctional Metrics

Criticism of the metrics used to evaluate good scholarship has been present throughout the whole period. However, the frequency and strength of such criticism has increased in recent years. The dysfunctions of the requirement to publish in top tier journals only were particularly addressed by Walsh and Shapiro, but they were also emphasized by others, including by Mowday in his 1996 address: "When asked how the sabbatical had gone, my colleague replied that it went great; he'd gotten a couple of 'hits'." Ireland commented: "This comprehensive and inclusive perspective of scholarship contrasts with the narrow view that scholarship is demonstrated primarily or perhaps even exclusively by publishing in refereed journals and, particularly, in Class A or top-tier refereed journals."

Smith, Shapiro, and Lee reflected on the arbitrariness of the metrics used. Shapiro criticized the present dominant norm that "Nothing but publication in 'A journals' is important, and thus should not be done."

> There is little agreement among reviewers about what is an acceptable contribution. (Smith)

> The pressure to publish in only A-journals affects what we as scholars write, cite, what outlets we seek, what we teach, what we provide of services, and our type of research design. The pressure to publish in A-journals affects not only the lives of scholars seeking tenured faculty positions, but also the lives of management scholars at all career phases.
>
> Moreover, since we are talking about management scholars' voices, the pressure to publish in A-journals also affects the progression of management science. (Shapiro)

> What constitutes a contribution can be determined only over time. (Smith)

> Scholarly contributions should be evaluated by the subsequent knowledge they inspire. Not judging value primarily by numbers of top-tier publications, citation counts, or similar meaningful but imperfect measures. (Lee)

Walsh and Tsui raised concerns about what metrics and publication pressure do to us as scholars. Tsui also raised concerns about how the metric system contributed to the destruction of our legitimacy as a research community.

> Responding to all of the rating and ranking initiatives in our world, we created an audit culture in our universities, one that can denigrate our scholarly motives. The team production of research, self-promotion, and even acts of scientific misconduct (for example fabrication, falsification, and plagiarism) can all be seen as a response to pressure to generate a high volume of cited research. (Walsh)

> Academy is filled with heartless researchers and teachers who focus on advancing their self-interested goal of promotion and tenure. (Tsui)

> The relentless rating and ranking of our work and, even more particularly, our schools' attempts to shine in these appraisals, distracts us from the real work of scholarship. Scholars are not immune from the pressure to produce a high volume of certain kinds of work.
> Author, journal and school rankings undermine the sacred nature of scholarship. (Walsh)

> To gain legitimacy, many new entrants to the research community (for example researchers in China and Brazil) are importing Anglo-Saxon research traditions for their research topics, methods, and theories, rather than developing indigenous knowledge that may require or produce new methods and new theories. (Tsui)

Lack of Relevance

A lack of concern for the relevance of our research and how we are being perceived by the business or practitioner community has been a repeated reflection by a majority of the presidents throughout the whole period. We lack a concern for the relevance of our work.

> There is a great divide between research and practice. Our work may even harm management practice. (Tsui)

> The gulf between the science and practice of management is widening. (Van de Ven)

> We must translate our research for managers and executives. (Hitt)

> The emphasis is now on knowledge production certified by publication in a very small number of elite journals. It will increasingly be seen as "counting angels dancing on the head of a pin", by the public, particularly by the organizations most important to our future. (Huff)

Many argued that we need to consider new strategic positions (Huff and Tsui), evidence-based learning (Rousseau), and programmatic research (Lee and DeNisi), and stated that our research makes the world a better place (Cummings and McGahan).

> We need a new strategic position closer to the knowledge production being carried on within the organizations we study. (Huff)

> We must make sure our research-based knowledge is relevant and useful. (Cummings)

> Evidence-based management means translating principles based on best evidence into organizational practices. (Rousseau)

> We inspire and enable a better world through our scholarship. (Tsui)

> It is our duty and responsibility to make sure that our knowledge makes the world a better place. (Cummings)

> There is a need for programmatic research that lead[s] us to say, "I am confident that we know a lot about this topic, and I'd feel good advising executives and managers to spend a lot of money implementing our ideas based on our research." (Lee)

> We need to do a better job of connecting our research to the world around us. We should encourage young scholars to develop coherent research programs. (DeNisi)

> We must grasp the implications of the problems around us, and use our multidisciplinary perspectives, collegiality, and engagement with practice to do work now that, in the future, we can look back on with real satisfaction, knowing that we improved the lives of everyone around us.
>
> Outcomes should reflect access, enfranchisement, well-being, pollution, and other important criteria that reflect true prosperity. (McGahan)

Some of the presidents argued for a virtuous circle stemming from the business–research interactions (Huff, Van de Ven, and Bartunek).

> The knowledge that researchers, teachers, consultants, and practitioners learn by themselves is different and partial. If it could be coproduced and combined in some novel ways, the results could produce a dazzling synthesis that could profoundly advance theory, teaching, and practice. (Van de Ven)

> Maybe research versus practice and its related dichotomies can be better thought of as tensions and dualities we all have in common, but that we express in different ways. (Bartunek)

Other past presidents (for example Lee and Smith) highlighted that our research and publications must have value for further research.

> I am not talking about the technical merits of good research but, instead, the focus on the contribution. However, only over time will the worth of most contributions be fully recognized. (Smith)

> The value of scholarly contributions should be evaluated by the subsequent knowledge they inspire. (Lee)

The Role of Institutions and Our Universities

Business schools are changing. The development and the consequences of university accreditations and academic ranking for engaged scholarship were addressed by some of the outgoing presidents, including Ireland, Shapiro, Walsh, and Adler.

> Universities and business schools worldwide face significant changes that affect our work as scholars, including the type of scholarship we undertake and how it is assessed. Some of these changes have roots in the external environment, whereas others originate internally from within our institutions.
> Business schools are changing—scrutiny. This competition has been intensified by the business school rankings published annually by Business Week and U.S. News and World Report. Who among us works in a business school in which these annual rankings are not a hot topic of discussion and concern, whether initiated by the dean, the business advisory council, alumni, or students? Jim March reminds us that when we lost the ability to rank business schools to the business press, so ended the stable order of things we have enjoyed for so many years.
> The demands on business school faculty have increased dramatically and are often in conflict with each other. There is more pressure to publish; more pressure to publish in top journals; and more pressure to publish in specific sets of journals. At the same time, there is more pressure to perform well in the classroom, more pressure to generate funding, and more pressure to develop courses, research programs, even curricula that are more socially conscious. (Ireland)

> Muting some voices to favor others is not consistent with how "intellectual contributions" are assessed by business school accreditation reviews and is not consistent with Boyer's (1990) description of engaged scholarship. (Shapiro)

> I do not need to tell anyone in our field about all of the many rating and ranking schemes that swirl about us. The list seems endless.
> Editors, authors, and university administrators alike track journals' impact factors. (Walsh)

These accreditations and rankings have unintended consequences.

> I see three unintended consequences of this ongoing emphasis on self-sustaining programs and rankings. First, the rankings may well direct many prospective students to our programs, both state supported and self-sustaining, which will help us both to fill classes and to reliably pay our bills. Second, many small, medium, large, and gigantic financial gifts are often directed toward the higher-ranked programs, which will also help us pay our bills. (Lee)

> The relentless rating and ranking of our work and, even more particularly, our schools' attempts to shine in these appraisals, distracts us from the real work of scholarship. Journal lists and rankings have stolen the sacredness of our scholarship. (Walsh)

Some argued that we cannot remain passive when seeing this development, and we need to "articulate [a] more viable vision of the role of the university" (Adler). "We have reproduced and internalized this audit culture in our own universities. I fear for our future if that culture is left unchecked" (Walsh).

One issue raised about ranking was short-termism in faculty evaluations.

> Looking critically at our institutional context, it is clear that we must also contend with challenges that come from within our faculty ranks. I would highlight in particular the damaging effect of the status hierarchy that elevates research over teaching, especially in the more research-intensive universities. As Ernest Boyer noted in 1990, teaching is given ever less consideration in the norms, values, and promotion and reward systems of our research-intensive universities. (Adler)

> Second, we need to pay attention to how we evaluate our senior colleagues. I cannot speak for all universities, but I fear that too many evaluate their faculty's performance on an annual basis. (Walsh)

> Judge and reward faculty on the basis of programmatic research and real contributions. (DeNisi)

Reframing International Dialogues

Several presidents raised concerns about the US-centricity developed through the global aspirations and developments of the AOM. This seems to be a main point of tension across the various past presidents. On one side there was a focus on becoming and developing a position as the global academy of management; on the other side, on being an international academy of management alongside other national or regional academies of management. A third position was that of being a global academy of management, but nurturing relationships with other academies.

The global aspiration was voiced by Glynn in particular, but also by others.

The strategic ambition for AOM that by 2022, the AOM will be the premier global community for management and organization scholars and for advancing the impact of management and organization science on business and society. (Glynn)

I would like to see the Academy of Management hold its annual meeting outside of the United States or Canada. I believe such an event would be a pivotal occasion in the life of our organization. (Hambrick)

That occasion will soon be upon us: the 2025 AOM annual meeting will be held in Copenhagen, Denmark. Can we pivot? (Glynn)

The focus on internationalization versus globalization was raised by various outgoing presidents, including Hitt, Starbuck, Van de Ven, DeNisi, and Tsui.

We must eliminate the US-phobic approach to management education and research. (Hitt)

I am impressed by the importance of dialectic processes for intellectual development.
    Scholars in different nations evolve semi-independent intellectual traditions. (Starbuck)

Our journals are dominated by North American-trained scholars, who share a specific model of how research should be conducted and reported. (DeNisi)

We do not seek to be a global academy of management and colonize the world. Rather, we seek to enlighten ourselves about our global profession and to confederate with associations throughout the world to accomplish this. (Van de Ven)

The trend towards homogenization in the research paradigm between Europe and North America and between Asia and North America is detrimental to the development of valid knowledge of contexts that are different from North America and Europe. (Tsui)

Warnings about the need for AOM's global leadership position were raised, particularly by DeNisi:

> We must connect our research to the world around us.
> We cannot assume that others would want AOM to be leaders in a global consortium, or even as participants in such an effort.
> In some ways, this challenge gets right to our identity as an organization. We call ourselves THE Academy of Management, but many members from other parts of the world refer to us as the American Academy of Management. In fact, I have been told by some international members that we can call ourselves whatever we want, but we will still be the American Academy of Management. Perhaps that is true. Perhaps our organization will always have an American flavor because this is the country where it was founded. But that doesn't mean we should accept that fact and move on. What do we aspire to be? Do we want to be an American or North American organization that simply has international members, or do we want to be a truly global organization? We need to decide. Likewise, we need to decide what the nature of the relationship will be between the Academy and its affiliates (such as the Ibero-American Academy) and associates (such as the European Academy, the Brazilian Academy, or EGOS (the European Group and Organization Studies Group). Early discussions in the strategic planning sessions seemed to point to a desire, on our part, to be leaders in a global consortium. Of course, that assumes that others would want us as leaders, or even as participants in such an effort. (DeNisi)

Creating a Sustainable Community of Scholars

Several presidents argued for the importance of community, for example Tung, Van de Ven, and Glynn. It is in AOM's mission statement to build a vibrant and supportive community of scholars. Some presidents raised concerns regarding the development of our community as scholars. Are we working together for each other or do we only think about ourselves? Is our community sustainable? Lee and DeNisi suggested team-based and programmatic research, Chen suggested that we should learn from Chinese values, and Ireland suggested that we should bring together scholars from across the world.

> Challenges and pressures for change faced by business schools are great. What are the implications for our scholarly values? On the one hand, we can view the pressures as a threat to our scholarly values. On the other hand, the

challenges we face might be viewed as a golden opportunity to reaffirm our scholarly values.

> This may sound like romantic madness if you think of the Academy as an instrumental organization, but it is our SOUL if you think of the Academy as a professional community. (Van de Ven)

Values of Chinese management scholars include the idea of community conversations.

> Our core values and guiding principles derive from the 'middle' or 'zhong' philosophy. (Chen)

"We must build social processes that foster interpersonal intimacy as an anecdote for organizational anomie—a fellowship among colleagues" (Whetten), and provide a "supportive and dynamic community for learning and sharing" (Van de Ven). We must "build a vibrant and supportive community of scholars" (Glynn). We must always "aspire to be better, human beings. We should share with one another what truly matters most" (Whetten). We must "build and foster a sustainable community within the Academy" (Tung).

> Bringing scholars together from across the world to collaboratively create knowledge, bring perspective to isolated and disparate facts, creatively apply knowledge in impactful ways, and actively disseminate knowledge to others. (Ireland)

> What does our scholarship reveal about community? (Glynn)

DeNisi raised a challenge by presenting the difference between the ideal scholarly community values and the dominant business community values.

> Science (and so academia) is seen as operating under a model of "the commons," where (1) information is shared openly and ideas are discussed freely, (2) validity is valued (i.e., not all ideas are equal), and (3) issues and answers are often complex. Business, on the other hand, operates under a model where (1) secrecy is valued, (2) there is an emphasis on results and utility, and (3) leaders need answers—not ambiguity. (DeNisi)

Importance of Passion and Compassion

Tung, Whetten, Bartunek, Smith, and Tsui focused on compassion, compassionate intellectuals, and educating the heart, not only publishing in top tier journals.

> Let's keep high standards for scholarship, encouraging passionate scholars to do their best work while maintaining an open mind about their unique contributions. Let's demonstrate more perspective, compassion, and empathy.
>   Be passionate about your ideas but be creative and pragmatic in presenting them to the market. (Smith)
>
> Compassion is essential for a sustainable future. (Tsui)
>
> We should balance educating the mind with educating the heart. (Tung)
>
> When we are judged only on how many papers we publish in certain journals and not on whether our research is important to society, we lose meaning in our work. (Tsui)

Cummings argued for engaged scholarship: AOM "is a community of practicing scholars. Engaged research might help us identify important variables and explanations not previously considered." Tsui stated: "Engaged scholarship means more compassionate research and less dispassionate research, and we need to restore compassion to our research and teaching activities."

Research for the Future

Some highlighted the importance of doing research for the future and to contribute to a better world. Bartunek presented her dreams for the future:

> I think that an underlying message of the dream is the possibility and the encouragement it holds out to us that our work—our individual work and that of the Academy—can be life giving for those of us who carry it out, for the Academy as a whole, and for our stakeholders. We really do have within us, as an Academy, the resources to make a positive difference in the world for the profession of management, the advancement of which is our primary mission.

We need to dare to care, and even fight, for what we believe in. Formulations like this were presented by, for example, von Glinow, Tung, and Tsui. Several presidents (such as Cummings, Walsh, Adler, and McGahan) raised the issue of committing to work toward a better world.

> We also need to develop, in doctoral students, an awareness that research findings and new ways of conceptualizing can and should make a difference for good in the world. (Bartunek)

> How can we respond to the changing societal and institutional context? (Adler)

> The most important phenomena of our time are unprecedented.
> We must extend our conceptualizations of validity and rigor, and elevate its epistemology.
> Three steps should be taken: First, liberalizing our empirical agenda. Second, a broader range of methodologies. Third, the theoretical foundations of the field of management need strengthening. (McGahan)

> One possible future outcome is a research agenda that accounts for both researchers' and practitioners' interests, one advancing scientific knowledge while helping to solve world problems. (Cummings)

> We should work in the interests of promoting solutions to the world's pressing problems. (McGahan)

THE AOM PRESIDENTS AND OUR SCHOLARLY ECOSYSTEM[4]

The global role and ambitions of AOM were presented and discussed in the addresses by several of the outgoing AOM presidents (Glynn, 2019; Starbuck, 1999; Van de Ven, 2002; DeNisi, 2010; Tsui, 2013). The AOM is a global trendsetter and benchmark in management research. It is a large and global association of scholars, and directly or indirectly, AOM is influencing scholarly practice. It is influencing institutions, the scholarly community, what is being studied, how research is being communicated, and who is being addressed in management research and scholarly activities. However, the AOM is also like a big tankship that has difficulty making turns or changing direction. AOM presently has a strong momentum, but the direction being attributed to AOM is not always in line with reflections from the AOM leadership and its presidents. It has therefore been important to explore some of the gaps

---

[4]   In the previous section, when referring to the addresses, I used the year in which they actually took place. In this section I refer to the written presentations in AMR, which appeared the following year.

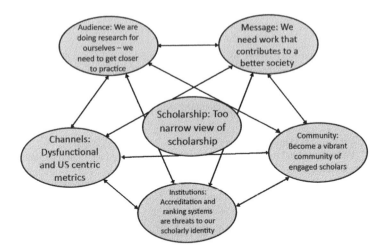

*Figure 3.1   Outgoing presidents' reflections positioned in the
scholarly ecosystem*

between the existing POP culture in management research that was presented in Chapter 2, and the ambitions of the former AOM presidents.
This has been done here in Chapter 3.

What were the contributions of these presidential addresses, and how
were they followed up? In Figure 3.1, I have positioned reflections from
the outgoing AOM presidents in the scholarly ecosystem that I presented
in Chapter 2.

Concerns about the Future and Efforts to Nurture True Scholarship

Several of the presidents emphasized passion and compassion as being
important for true scholarship (Bartunek, 2003; Smith, 2008; Tsui, 2013;
Tung, 2005; Whetten, 2001). The presidents had concerns about the
development of the role of scholars, and scholarly development. Our
view of scholarship is too narrow. The concerns regarding the future of
academia, the future of scholars, the future of the profession, and the
future of universities and business schools were there across the period,
but the serious concern regarding the POP culture and the urgent need to
nurture true scholarship seem to be growing. The presidents are raising
new issues over time, but they are also building on the concerns previ-

ously presented. The urgency to do something increasingly comes forth. Many of the outgoing presidents returned to Hambrick's address and reflected on Boyer's definition of scholarship. This was also reflected in the former presidents' panel at the AOM annual conference in Chicago in 2018.

Institutions—Who Is Setting the Standards?

There was a concern for the role of institutions and our universities and business schools. They are changing, and not only in positive ways. The changes are presenting challenges for true scholarship, and are setting standards for the content and audience of our research, for publication and dissemination policy, and for the development of the academic community. There is concern that accreditation and ranking systems are becoming threats to our scholarly identity. This was already presented by Mowday (1997), and followed up later by, for example, Tung (2005) and DeNisi (2010), as well as by Walsh (2011) and Adler (2016). Collegiums should be built from the bottom up.

The assessment and audit culture might be seen as a problem. The present audit culture might be harmful to society.

Audience—For Whom Do We Research?

Our responsibility is not to ourselves, but to the world we live in (Glynn, 2019). Several of the former presidents argued that theory and practice are not connected. We must get closer to practice. Management research should not only contribute to a scientific discipline, but also advance the practice of management (Tsui, 2013; Van de Ven, 2002). Any academic field that exists to satisfy only itself and its own interests will soon have few resources (Hambrick, 1994: 16). We should help businesses and individuals doing business (Hitt, 1998). Rousseau (2006) suggested that evidence-based learning provides a model that may close the research–practice gap. Finally, Tsui (2013: 176) warned about the self-interested goals of promotion and tenure.

Message—What Do We Communicate?

Many of the former AOM presidents were critical of the evolving narrow view of scholarship. They noted that definitions of scholarship have narrowed over time (Mowday, 1997: 338). "Scholarship has become to present publishing research in refereed journals, rather than the broader search for and dissemination and application of new knowledge." There is a need to see the whole, not only holes. We should immerse head, heart, and hands, and have an engaged and holistic thoughtful view, based on maturity and diversity (Bartunek, 2003; Cummings, 2007; Tsui, 2013; Van de Ven, 2002; Whetten, 2001).

Some presented the need to do research for the future, including initiatives to address some of the great challenges the world is facing. Several argued that we should "dare to care" (von Glinow, 1996; Tsui, 2013; Tung, 2005), and address our research to making a better society (Adler, 2016; Bartunek, 2003; Cummings, 2007; McGahan, 2018).

Channels—How Do We Disseminate Our Knowledge?

A major, and increasing, concern was that we adapt to metrics that are dysfunctional and US-centric, and that this culture creates a system of publishing technicians (Shapiro, 2017; Walsh, 2011). Walsh argued that research questions, methods, and samples are often shaped by choice of journal. Publications are only a minor part of doing research. Scholarship is the broader search for and dissemination of knowledge and applications. Research should be conducted on topics where there is a need, and using appropriate methods. There should be second and third order effects, communicated through mentoring and tutoring. A win-at-all-costs culture has developed. This culture might contribute to the rise of scientific misconduct and wrongdoing that concerns so many these days (Walsh, 2011).

Community—What Is Characterizing Us?

The presentation of what should characterize us as a community was described in three partly overlapping points. It should be a sharing community: communal, open, and impact-driven. Several presidents argued for the importance of this (Glynn, 2018; Tung, 2005; Van de Ven, 2002). This community should foster interpersonal intimacy (Whetten, 2001). Some argued for a sharing and vibrant community with mutual respect, reciprocity, and enduring relationships, and that we as scholars should share with one another what truly matters, engage in community conversations, and have a willingness as individual members to share with one another. The community should be openminded, supporting team-based research to conduct programmatic scholarship, and educate members about the value of adopting different research models (DeNisi, 2010; Lee, 2009; Smith, 2008).

We should develop a community that enables collective action and change (Glynn, 2019). Senior faculty should strive to improve the research environment for junior faculty so they can realize their intellectual ideals and become the best they can be (Chen, 2014; Tsui, 2013; Whetten, 2001). The time horizon for this is our entire academic life (Bartunek, 2003). We need personal engagement and job engagement displayed by the use of head, heart, and hands (Shapiro, 2017). We need a society that goes beyond "winner takes all."

Research will benefit from interaction and from us learning from each other. Ideas and possibilities will then develop. The community should be impact-driven, with compassion and a focus on a sustainable future and educating minds with educating hearts, always aspiring to be better human beings. Doctoral students should be challenged to find their calling and follow their hearts (Tsui, 2013; Whetten, 2001: 178).

DEVELOPING A VIBRANT AND SUSTAINABLE COMMUNITY

The rest of the book is dedicated to the presentation of ways of creating a vibrant and sustainable community of scholars. It is about resolving the crisis in research by changing the game. The AOM has been presented as a big tankship with major momentum, and it may be difficult to change its direction and speed. The European Academy of Management (EURAM) is one of several similar associations, and I can see how EURAM and other smaller associations can contribute, as tugboats, in adjusting the direction of the big tankship. This is presented in Chapter 4. In Chapter 5, I return to the ecosystem and present many of the initiatives that now are being taken to resolve the crisis and change the ecosystem equilibrium from a POP culture to a true scholarship culture.

In the second part of the book, I present some of my experiences in developing a sharing philosophy for creating vibrant and sustainable communities of scholars. I suggest a new game. In Chapter 6, I present the plan with a focus on a communal approach; in Chapter 7 I have a focus on open innovation and openmindedness, including the presentation of a lighthouse that may guide the tankship and the tugboats. In Chapter 8, I present an impact-driven approach with a focus on working with stakeholders. In all three chapters, I present and demonstrate ways in which the concepts and suggestions presented in Chapter 5 can be applied.

Contributions from the whole book are discussed and summarized in Chapter 9. In Chapter 10 I offer a short conclusion about a sharing philosophy, resolving the crisis in research and "Ritorno al passato": returning to the past—returning to true scholarship.

4. What about EURAM?

EXPANDING THE AOM SPHERE: NATIONAL AND REGIONAL ACADEMIES

> The scholars in different nations evolve semi-independent intellectual traditions. For instance, population ecology is popular in the United States, structuration in Britain, postmodern deconstruction in France, and longitudinal case studies in Scandinavia. These differences often nurture claims of superiority and allegations of irrelevance. In my experience, however, the existence of sharply contrasting views has always turned out to be a sign that neither side is wrong and that both sides have validity. We gain more, I think, if we regard each intellectual tradition as having value to contribute and as deserving of respect.
>
> (Starbuck, 1999: 190)

The inaugural meeting of the European Academy of Management (EURAM) took place in Barcelona in April 2001. Such an association had been considered for some time, but the direct initiative for this association was taken by the European Institute for Advanced Studies in Management (EIASM). EIASM had earlier founded similar associations, for example in accounting. EIASM and EURAM are associations for scholars. A European association for business schools and universities teaching management had already been established through the European Foundation for Management Development (EFMD). A pan European organization for scholars doing organization studies (EGOS) also existed, and EGOS was considered to be the main European alternative to an academy of management. EGOS was embedded in European cultures, and its relationship with the US-based Academy of Management (AOM) had been characterized by constraints, and even hostility.

In Europe, there also existed various national or regional academies of management, for example the British Academy of Management (BAM), the Nordic Academy of Management (NFF), the Italian Academy of Management (AIDEA), the French Academy of Management (AIMS), the German Academy of Management (VHB), and the Central and

Eastern European Academy of Management (CEEMAN).[1] Scholarly associations of management have also been established on other continents, some of them as affiliates of AOM: examples of these include the Iberoamerican Academy of Management, the Indian Academy of Management (INDAM), the Asia Academy of Management (AAOM), and the African Academy of Management (AFAM). Others are independent, such as the International Association for Chinese Management Research (IACMR) and the Australian and New Zealand Academy of Management (ANZAM). Many of the academies of management were established as early as the 1980s or 1990s. There also existed a federation for all academies of management, the International Federation of Scholarly Associations of Management (IFSAM).

In establishing EURAM, EIASM had invited some of the most noted scholars from different European countries to form a EURAM executive committee. Some of them had a background from EGOS, others from AOM. Some were simply featured professors at leading business schools in their actual country. Those with an EGOS background typically had a skeptical attitude toward AOM, and often also toward EGOS.

In 1999, Bill Starbuck, past president of AOM, took me aside at the AOM annual meeting. He foresaw growth in AOM's membership coming as a result of scholars from outside the US, anticipating that the growth in members from the US would soon be outnumbered by the growth in those coming from other countries. The US membership had started to stagnate. I was then Director of the International Programs Committee (IPC) at AOM. He wanted to discuss with me the possibility of establishing a European affiliate of AOM. He considered that the time was ripe to establish a European Academy of Management. I was skeptical.

Carolyn Dexter, the founder of the IPC at AOM, was highly involved in IFSAM. Carolyn, who died in 1999, saw the IFSAM as an umbrella organization and a meeting place for scholars and scholarly associations around the world. Around 2000, as the AOM board discussed ceasing its membership of IFSAM, I strongly argued against that. I saw IFSAM as a possible meeting place for leaders of scholarly associations of management. As a member of the IPC, for several years I had analyzed AOM's non-US participation and membership. I had also carried out various membership surveys about what it means to be international, and to

---

[1]   Some of them, for example CEEMAN, have taken steps to work also outside their original region.

my surprise, I had found that many of the US members were concerned about the growth in international membership and attention. There were voices among the US members raising the need for a national AOM that could pay attention to the needs of US scholars, and not only think internationally.

In 2001, Dave Whetten was past president of AOM. I was still Director of the IPC (later called International Themes Committee—ITC) at AOM, and I had worked closely with Dave. We discussed the inaugural meeting of EURAM, and he asked me to go there and represent AOM. No other formal AOM officer would be there. I took with me a positive attitude both to the development of EURAM and to AOM.

I continued my EURAM membership and conference participation, and in 2009, to my surprise, I was elected as EURAM's third president. I was elected as president for a period of two years—from 2010 to 2012. My positive attitude to the AOM and its leadership continued, but I also observed many of the difficulties and challenges arising from the European scholars' growing veneration of AOM and the publishing techniques communicated.

IS THERE A NEED FOR A EUROPEAN-BASED ACADEMY?

There are many regional and national academies of management, with varying visions and ambitions, and their relations to the AOM influence have also varied. In Europe, the sentiment toward the AOM from many members of EGOS and EURAM has in recent decades moved from one of hostility to one of adoration. In other regions and countries, we have seen a movement from adoration to caution. Awareness of contextualization has been increasing, for example by observing that traditional management cultures, philosophies, and traditions have been given little attention.

Europe represents the beauty and difficulties of diversity. The "lingua Franca" in management research is now English. However, the majority of scholars in Europe have a mother tongue and teaching language other than English. Challenges developed in one language cannot always be communicated in other languages.

Is there a need for European-based research? What does it mean that most European scholars do not have English as their mother tongue? Are there distinct topics and issues which Europe and European countries need to address? What about empirical data from Europe or European countries? Are these of interest in US-based journals? How are the European variations in research and academic traditions being understood and appreciated in an American-based globalization of scholarship? Can a European-based academy contribute as an alternative to the monopoly situation in which AOM is about to find itself?

I will answer yes to all these questions. European scholars are facing challenges other than those typically addressed at AOM. Europe and European countries represent different contextual conditions than those easily addressed in a US-based global setting. If we consider a global academy of management, I could see the AOM as a big tankship whose direction is difficult to change. EURAM and other academies of management may be seen as making a contribution as tugboats that may support the big boat in understanding variations in the local waters. Severe damage or disaster may easily occur without interaction between the big vessel and the local tugboats. Independent tugboats may have a greater impact than various national and regional boats following in the aftermath of the big tanker.

I considered all the above reflections as EURAM president. I saw EURAM as an instrument for a larger purpose, and I was willing to merge it with other organizations if that would be beneficial for contributing to the above questions. The practical side of this was that I also initiated discussions with Eero Vaara, as EGOS president, and the EGOS board on finding ways we could collaborate. I also actively followed up discussions with Jim Walsh, AOM president in this period. Furthermore, during our annual conferences EURAM created a meeting place for presidents of other associations of management. These presidential activities are still important program items at EURAM's annual conferences.

Some other European-initiated associations downplayed the role of the "E" in their names, such as the European Group of Organisation Studies (EGOS), European Foundation for Management Development (EFMD), and European Association for Business in Society (EABIS). This made it even more important to maintain and develop a European-based Academy of Management. This was also one of my reasons, as EURAM president and a believer in the need for a European-based academy of management, for advising AOM against holding their meetings outside North America. I saw this as a shortsighted and hostile initiative.

CREATING A EUROPEAN BASED COMMUNITY OF ENGAGED MANAGEMENT SCHOLARS[2]

In 2010, I held an address as EURAM president. This was published in *European Management Review* (EMR) (Huse, 2010: 133–5). In this address, I presented my vision as incoming president of EURAM. The address was as follows:

After 20 years of active membership at the Academy of Management in the US, I have personally seen the need for an organization in Europe that can have some of AOM's community-building meeting place functions. I attended the first EURAM meeting and represented then the Academy of Management—being its Director of International Programs/Themes. We can learn much from the USA, but there are some challenges and possibilities in Europe that cannot be met by only adapting to the US research standards.

In the ballot for the presidential election in 2009, I presented some mission statements or ambitions, which were as follows:

- Direction and objective: To develop EURAM into a European-based community of management scholars having meeting place functions similar to those of the US Academy of Management, including the professional development workshops in which particular European issues may be emphasized.
- EURAM identity: To initiate developments among the members, officers and the board in EURAM to increase organizational identity.
- Internal organization: To continue the efforts of developing Strategic Interest Groups (SIG) at EURAM, as they may contribute to continuity and organizational accumulation of knowledge.
- High-quality journal: To give high priority to the development of the European Management Review (EMR).

Meeting Needs

There is a need for a EURAM conference that has some of the meeting-place functions found at the US Academy of Management. However, in EURAM, we should focus even more on diversity and the

---

[2]   This section was previously published in Huse (2010), pp.133–5. Some minor adjustments have been made, such as changes to paragraph titles.

international and crosscultural perspectives in research and practice which are at the core of the European setting. We need a community of engaged scholars that is there to serve the needs of European businesses, voluntary organizations, and public policy practices. We need a community that can nurture the strength and develop the possibilities of European research and academic traditions: one that meets the requirements of European scholars needing to overcome language challenges, heterogeneous and sometimes small job markets, and a large variety of educational backgrounds and academic requirements. To this community we welcome members from all over the world. The annual conference will most likely be a core meeting place in the future; the conference should not only be a place for presenting high-quality research but should also be a meeting place for focusing on possibilities including professional development and job market activities.

EURAM and the annual conference should facilitate networks for the dialogue between scholars, reflective practitioners, and policymakers. It also gives our members an occasion to create, develop and renew professional and social relationships. It will be given high priority to develop the conferences in such a way that the community-building objectives will be met. This may have consequences for the selection of conference sites and conference organization.

EURAM faces a challenge in contributing to developing and communicating professional standards among its members coming from a large variety of national academic backgrounds. An understanding of professional standards and ethics is essential. These standards often vary across countries, as what may be important in, for example, the USA may not necessarily fit the situations in Europe. In Europe, there are various traditions for professor–student relationship, academic accreditations and appointments, conducting and funding research, and ways of publishing. Thus, EURAM has the main task of providing professional development activities to doctoral students and junior faculty. They are the future, and I will make it a priority to support them in finding their academic home at EURAM, to help them understand the challenges and possibilities in European research traditions and to help them become engaged scholars. There has been a good tradition at the EURAM conferences to have a doctorial colloquium. I hope to see this tradition continue and develop so as to meet junior faculty needs, and that many of these professional development activities should be organized by the SIGs.

Organizational Identity—Engaged Community

One of the biggest challenges for EURAM is to increase its organizational identity—my observation has been that members still only have a limited feeling of ownership and identification in relation to the organization. Creating pride and organizational identity among the members was included in the mission statements presented in the ballot.

I still see the importance of creating a EURAM identity among the members. EURAM is not only a provider of an academic conference, but also an organization working for its members and the management research community and stakeholders. This requires a community engaged in the exercise of EURAM's mission statement. An ownership relationship and EURAM identification should be developed among members at all levels, not only among the Board and Executive Committee members.

The members should consider EURAM as one of their academic homes—a place where they meet colleagues, friends, and academic possibilities, stimulations, and challenges. In creating an academic home, it is also important for the President and the Executive Committee to emphasize respect, predictability, involvement, some kind of idealism, and a commitment to high quality.

Open, Inclusive, International, and Crosscultural Community

Diversity and respect for variations in background are the main needs while developing a European-based community of scholars, and should be a cornerstone in the EURAM identity. EURAM should be characterized by being an open, inclusive, international, and crosscultural community. This should be reflected in all EURAM activities and throughout the whole organization. Another aspect I strongly emphasize in the EURAM identity is engaged scholarship and ethical conduct in anything we are doing.

It was indicated in the introduction of this vision and mission statement that my involvement with EURAM is not because of a desire to develop an organization. My involvement and willingness to serve exists because I see that there are needs to be met. This will also have implications for the direction I believe EURAM should take in the future. Meeting needs is not only a question about urgent immediate action—neither to meet immediate needs nor to use opportunities. In the case of the direction for EURAM development, it is also about understanding the longer-term evolution of the academic, business, and political environments of which we are part. Meeting these needs should be a joint concern for all of us, and as the President of EURAM, I will be very happy with all kinds of input. However, regardless of the direction EURAM will take, anything we are doing should be characterized by engaged scholarship and high professional standards. This is a challenge for all of us.

CONTEXT-SPECIFIC RESEARCH

In Chapter 3 I highlighted that in their AOM Presidential Addresses, Starbuck (1999), Tung (2005), DeNisi (2010), Walsh (2011), and Ireland (2015) all emphasized the importance for AOM of listening to and learning from learned societies outside the US, and Hitt (1998) argued for the need to eliminate the US-centric approach to management research. Van de Ven (2002) and Chen (2014) are among those who focused on the need for context-specific research.

Andrew van de Ven followed up my address presented in the previous section. In a reflection paper in EMR on creating a community of engaged scholars (van de Ven, 2011), he highlighted the importance of doing indigenous research in diverse European countries and cultures. This was a result of his growing recognition of "an understanding of the importance of, and identity with, context-specific management issues and problems in local European countries, but also for advancing general theoretical knowledge across cultural boundaries" (Van de Ven, 2011: 189). Using the term "indigenous research," he referred to Tsui (2004: 501), who defined this as "scientific studies of local phenomena using local language, local subjects and locally meaningful constructs, with the aim to test or build theories that can explain and predict the specific phenomenon in the local cultural context."

Van de Ven argued that we should not homogenize management research by adapting and applying foreign theories that are not sensitive to local contexts. The importance of non-American scholarly communities had to be captured. Some important themes that needed to be addressed were that the scholarly community is pluralistic (not monolithic), that indigenous research needs to be encouraged and conducted, and that imitating the American brand of research throughout the world is creating a deterioration in management knowledge. At stake is the need for variations in the evolutionary development of scientific management knowledge. The quality and growth of scientific knowledge suffer when management scholarly communities adopt a homogeneous brand of research methods and outputs that are unable to create the variations necessary for future adaptability and survival.

We should instead stimulate diversity or heterogeneity by developing local management theories, methods, and institutions. It is so easy to apply and be influenced by the methods in which we are trained. From his stance in a western positivistic research tradition, van de Ven (2011) argued that we often do not inquire into or appreciate the unique cultural values, interests, and knowledge inherent in what we are studying. Without understanding the local traditions, we often fail to understand that there may be negative obstructive effects of "foreign" research methods.

Referring to Boyer (1996b), van de Ven argued for the need for context-specific research to understand the phenomenon and its boundary conditions. Many issues require the views of scholarly leaders from various parts of the world, such as those involved in EURAM, EGOS, the Iberoamerican Academy of Management, and others:

> Engaged scholarship begins with a humble appreciation that the indigenous topics being studied typically exceed our limited individual capabilities. As a result, in order to better understand the topic being studied, we need to step outside of ourselves and engage with relevant stakeholders. It requires researchers to become participants in a collective learning process and to be reflexive of whose perspectives and interests are served in a study. (Van de Ven, 2011: 194)

PRESIDENTIAL ACTIVITIES—TUGBOATS PREPARED TO SUPPORT

At EURAM's annual conference in 2011, presidents of various learned associations of management were invited to share and discuss challenges and problems in our research communities, and the future of management research. This followed up on an agreement at an event at the AOM conference in 2010, led by AOM past president Jim Walsh. EURAM then offered to support AOM to jointly meet challenges we face as learned associations of management. As mentioned above, these presidential activities have since continued as a permanent part of EURAM's annual conference program.

The presidential activities at EURAM in 2011 and 2012 showed much of the beauty and difficulties of diversity in traditions and practice. EURAM had to balance many perspectives about what true scholarship is. It was clearly displayed that there is not one homogeneous way of thinking. During these meetings, I was personally influenced by my AOM background.

One of the key issues discussed at the presidential activities at EURAM's meetings in 2011 and 2012 was journal lists and rankings. The Association of Business Schools (ABS) in the UK had invited EURAM and other learned associations to become coowners of the ABS list of journal rankings, and thus also to introduce the ABS list as a European standard for evaluation of publications. The British Academy of Management (BAM) representatives strongly warned against this list, and so did the representatives of the French Academy of Management (AIMS). The ABS list became a starting point for various arguments. It was argued that the universities might want lists to monitor and give incentives for research activities, but that such lists are negative for scholars. Scholars should be evaluated not based on where they publish, but based on their contributions. The discussions reflected disagreement among European scholars as to how and whether European countries and universities should follow a US-based tenure track system that could lead to a publish or perish (POP) culture.

As EURAM president in this period, I also wanted to meet my commitment to the scholarly society and to find alternatives to the globalization of the US-based tenure track system. In 2010 I had told Jim Walsh and AOM that EURAM could work as a tugboat that can help the big tankship change its direction away from this POP culture.

REFLECTIONS FROM AN OUTGOING EURAM PRESIDENT

After my two-year period as EURAM president, I gave my reflective outgoing presidential speech in 2012. The speech was published in EURAM's newsletter (Huse, 2012a: 1–3). An extract follows:[3]

> Dear EURAM members, friends and colleagues. One of the things I have appreciated the most during my period as president is the overwhelming support for the EURAM strategy and the commitment I made, as I was a candidate for becoming the president. The support I got from you as individual members and from sister organizations: EURAM should be a European based

---

[3]   A few typographical adjustments have been made to the cited text from the newsletter.

community of engaged management scholars, and that EURAM exists to meet needs among scholars, businesses and the society at large.

Working as a president has been extremely rewarding, but also extremely time consuming and resource demanding. Attending meetings of our sister organizations almost once a month, working directly with highly committed and motivated volunteers including with the various strategic interest groups (SIGs) and their officers, contributing to shaping the future of management research, and meeting so many positive persons. Here I will highlight some of my reflections on a few issues that in these two years have been given priority: community building, establishing engaged scholarship and having a European based platform, external relations and academic assessments.

Community building and engaged scholarship

EURAM is not only a conference, but also a community supporting and nurturing scholars and scholarships. Long-term membership and continuity in the SIGs will follow. The individual members and the SIGs will be the core units in the community, and our attention should go to stimulating and supporting the development of the SIGs. Furthermore, the community should be built on involvement and voluntarism. In the community, we shall not have somebody serving the rest, but all should be there for each other. Active initiatives need to be taken for securing inclusion and involvement at all levels. Inclusion involves in the short run much planning and direct contacts. However, much more work is needed. The resources of EURAM are and shall be a caring community, scholarly contribution and voluntarism. EURAM may have and need financial resources to be able to achieve some of the goals, but our real resources are and should be the competencies and involvement of our members.

Engaged scholars believe in what they are doing, which also includes a deep or deeper level rigor and relevance. We shall enjoy being able to publish, and we shall be involved in developing good journals and outlets for our research. We may also need to develop and stimulate outlets and journals that are different from already existing outlets. We need journals and other outlets focusing deep level relevance and deep level rigor—focusing on our needs and challenges in Europe. However, publishing should never be the final objective of our efforts. I want to see scholars wanting to contribute to knowledge creation—directly or through others. I want to see scholars that believe in what they are doing—both with respect to rigor and to relevance—a deep level rigor and deep level relevance that is important for knowledge creation and meeting needs in the society. We should rethink the objective of our doctoral programs and academic training. We should train our student so that they can have contributions in academia, business and society—also for future generations. Our students are the future, and how we train them will have implications for the future of our societies. Top scholarship is not only related to publications in US based journals, but about maturity and contributions.

European based and a forum for external relations

We need to focus on Europe and not having the ambition of conquering the whole world, but at the same time, we should be inspired by what takes place on other continents. I have during my presidency been happy to share with colleagues and similar organization on other continents. However, EURAM must never forget or be distracted from our objectives. We need to have an understanding and perspectives going beyond local issues in Europe. However, our core is in Europe, European based research and European based scholars, and we are and should remain being a European based community. In a similar way AOM (USA) and ANZAM (Australia and New Zealand), etc have and should have it focus on their members from their region and have a main focus on meeting needs or raising questions of particular importance locally or regionally.

In Tallinn at the conference last year, and now in Rotterdam, we have guests or official representations from about twenty sister organizations. This forum, including several meetings during our conference and many follow up meetings, contributes to joint understanding and joint efforts in working for joint overarching objectives.

We believe and we see that our efforts are meaningful, and when standing together we can make a change. Through the external relations initiatives, we are finding our place and contribution in relation to other learned societies. Following up these relations has led me almost twice a month this year to attend meetings and conferences of other associations. However, they have helped us define our place and contribution in the international community. How can we make a contribution? Focus on collaboration rather than competition. The external relations have been in two main directions: Inside Europe and on the global arena. Personally, I will like to give IFSAM (International Federation of Scholarly Associations of Management) an important role in coordination among learned societies on the global arena, but I want to see IFSAM as an umbrella for collaborations among scholarly associations of management and not as a conference organizer.

Academic assessments and how to evaluate academic merit

This has been the content in many of the interactions and a strategic issue shaping EURAM's and also my decision-making. After a period of adapting to a system where academic assessment has been based on publications in a few US based journals, we have recently experienced a growing criticism of this fast approaching and more and more dominating pressure to publish, leading to an overly focus on publishing techniques rather than academic and scholarly maturity. Scholars in Europe have during the recent decade, gone through a process where we have learnt to publish and we have learnt many of the techniques of the handicraft of publishing. Now we need to set standards that are important on the European arena and for Europe, and we should also contribute to setting standards important for the global arena. We have a role in influencing standard settings. This can be done directly in relation to universities, country standards, etc. This can be done through involvement with or through various sister organizations as EFMD (European Foundation for Management Development), AOM (Academy of Management in USA) and through national and regional associations in Europe. I am very happy to see and learn from the development in Britain and at BAM (the British Academy of Management) and in various leading universities in Europe. Contributions and maturity more than only publications are again getting attention. On these issues, I have also been highly inspired by the French Academy of Management (AIMS) and in particular Thomas Durand. EMR (European Management Review) is EURAM's own journal, and important steps for raising its reputation have been made by its editor Alfonso Gambardella.

EURAM 2019 AND A NEW GAME FOR MANAGEMENT RESEARCH

As I completed work on this chapter, the EURAM 2019 annual conference had just been held in Lisbon, Portugal. During this conference, former EURAM presidents were invited to a panel discussing responsible research in business and management (RRBM). All highlighted the danger of the existing POP culture and raised the importance of true scholarship.

During the conference Sibel Yamak, EURAM president 2016–18, offered to read this chapter about EURAM. She concluded: "After reading your chapter I am more confident that EURAM is progressing in a very healthy and meaningful way." EURAM has now a policy that every conference proposal should relate to at least one of the United Nations Sustainable Development Goals. EURAM is becoming more and more sensitive to business and society issues.

AOM was not represented in EURAM's presidential activities in 2019.

During EURAM's 2019 General Assembly meeting, it was announced that separate committees would be established to address the issues of how we as management scholars may meet the grand societal challenges, and how to create a new game in doing management research—how to resolve the crisis in management research. It was also announced that EURAM's annual conference in 2021 would take place in Montreal in Canada.

5. Initiatives for changing the ecosystem equilibrium

INITIATIVES TO CHANGE THE POP CULTURE— CALLS FOR COORDINATED ACTION

We need coordinated action by key actors if we want to change the equilibrium of the scholarly ecosystem. In this chapter I will present some of the key actors and their actions and contributions. The motivation of all actors is to redirect the present publish or perish (POP) culture, to get back to meaning and true scholarship. They want to resolve the crisis in research.

"How can we take advantage of both predicted and unpredicted 'exogenous shocks' to guide academia towards producing scholarship that is the most value to 21st century society?" This is the question raised by Adler and Harzing (2009: 89), and is a core question in this chapter. Several initiatives have been undertaken in recent decades to show the need for rethinking scholarship, and many warnings have been given. A number of initiatives and suggestions regarding how to change the system can be found. The initiatives vary depending on the persons or institutions behind them, with variations in disciplinary and geographical backgrounds and traditions, differences in types of actions, and variations in purpose or objectives. In this chapter, I present some of these initiatives and analyze how they contribute to changing the equilibrium in a POP culture ecosystem. This is illustrated in Figure 5.1.

In the following, I will use an outline with a focus on how various parts of the ecosystem are approached. I do not aspire to present all initiatives, just some of those that have inspired me most. The initiatives are sorted according to some of the core elements in the ecosystem. However, most of them address more than one element—but that is also a typical ecosystem characteristic. Furthermore, it is important to identify the characteristics of the various initiating actors, the types of initiative they are taking, and the global or disciplinary variations that they may represent.

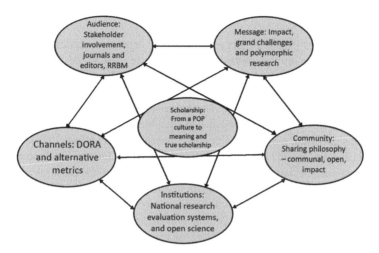

Figure 5.1   Initiatives to change the system

While writing this book, I was, to my surprise, nominated to become a member of the board of governors of Academy of Management (AOM). After some reflection, I accepted the nomination and was willing to run for this position. In the election ballot presentation, I wrote that my research and teaching are characterized by mentorship, including a sharing and open philosophy. I also wrote that I have signed the DORA declaration and endorsed the RRBM call. I do not know if this contributed to the election results, but I was elected, and I will have to bring these commitments with me as a representative-at-large member of the AOM board of governors.

INSTITUTIONS—SEARCHING A SUSTAINABLE SYSTEM FOR ASSESSING RESEARCH AT UNIVERSITIES AND BUSINESS SCHOOLS

Initiatives to change institutions can take place at several levels, for example through national evaluation systems, transnational regulations, accreditation agencies, and various private or voluntary endeavors stemming from DORA and RRBM. However, institutional impacts happen over time, and if impact is to be analyzed or assessed, it needs to be understood in a holistic way.

National Research Evaluation Systems

Evaluation systems for higher education exist in many countries. National research evaluation systems typically require systematic ranking of journals, scholars, and academic institutions. The British Research Excellence Framework (REF) is such a system.[1] The UK has been considered a leader in developing national research evaluation systems, but these systems have developed at considerable cost. They have also had some significant, negative unintended consequences (Moosa, 2018).

REF was in 2011 published by the Higher Education Research Council of England (HEFCE) and was conducted in 2014. A new assessment (REF2021) will be made in 2021. The objective of the REF framework was to be a means for national resource allocation, to assess quality—a mechanism for cultural change in academia. REF should produce robust UK-wide indicators of research excellence, to provide a basis for distributing funding, avoid undesirable behavioral incentives, and promote equality and diversity. REF is carried out by panels of senior academics, international members, and research users. Three distinct elements are being assessed—quality of output, impact beyond academia, and the environment that supports research.

Pettigrew (2011), upon the 25th anniversary of the British Academy of Management (BAM), argued that British research assessments right back to the mid-1980s have changed individual and institutional behavior. He made a list of several changes for inclusion in the evaluation of universities and business schools:

> a more open border between science and society, a stronger scientific independence, no unitary view science and no linear definition of the scientific process, involvement of stakeholders in the knowledge development process and greater pluralism in the research practice, a greater recognition of the localized character of research practice and outcomes, and a recognition of the complex interactions between multiple stakeholders in the research process and a more challenged view for evaluating the quality and relevance of research. (Pettigrew, 2011: 348)

The REF2021 assessment will emphasize public engagement more than what was the case in 2014. Public engagement goes beyond impact and

---

[1]   See http://www.ref.ac.uk/about/ for the UK REF initiatives.

dissemination. Public engagement is described in REF2021 as mutually beneficial interactions between researchers and citizens.

Open Science: FAIR and EU Open Access Initiatives[2]

"Open science" involves initiatives to make scientific research and its dissemination accessible. Open science highlights transparent and accessible knowledge and that science should be shared and developed through collaborative networks. Six main principles for open science are suggested (Kraker et al., 2011): open methodology, open source, open data, open access, open peer review, and open educational resources. Open data and open access are presently receiving major attention. They encompass practices such as publishing open research practices, encouraging the availability of research data, campaigning for open access, and generally encouraging scientists to make it easier to publish and communicate scientific knowledge.

The FAIR principles are part of the open science discussion. They are a set of guidelines to ensure that data, or any digital object, are findable, accessible, interoperable, and reusable. A community of scholars, librarians, archivists, publishers, journals, and research funders supports this initiative. The objective is to facilitate the change toward improved knowledge creation and sharing. Individually and collectively, the FAIR principles aim to bring about a change in modern scholarly communications through the effective use of information technology.

The "open access" requirements are another step in the direction of open science. The global shift toward making research findings available free of charge for readers has been a core strategy in the European Commission to improve knowledge circulation and thus innovation. In 2012, the European Commission encouraged all EU member states to put publicly funded research results in the public sphere in order to make science better and strengthen their knowledge-based economy. A group of national funders, joined by the European Commission and the European Research Council, has also announced plans to make open access publishing mandatory for recipients of their agencies' research funding. Open access means immediate, irrevocable, unrestricted, and

---

[2]   See   https://libereurope.eu/wp-content/uploads/2017/12/LIBER-FAIR -Data.pdf for the FAIR principles and https://ec.europa.eu/programmes/ horizon2020/en/h2020-section/open-science-open-access for EU open science initiatives, both accessed September 17, 2019.

free online access for any user worldwide to information products, and to unrestricted reuse of content. This coalition of national funders is dedicated to disseminating scholarly work as rapidly and widely as possible.

The background for the open science initiatives is the desire for scientists to have access to shared resources, while the experienced reality is that individual entities profit by controlling the availability of these resources. The FAIR principles and the open access requirements have direct consequences for universities and other research and higher education institutions, as they force them to rethink existing incentives and reporting practices. Publishers and journals are also forced to rethink their practice.

The library at my institution—BI Norwegian Business School—has developed the BI Research Depository (BIRD) to meet the FAIR principles (findable, accessible, interoperable, and reusable). In practice, this means that the data collected in my major research projects are available at BIRD.

AUDIENCE—NOT ONLY FOR A NARROW GROUP OF SCHOLARS, BUT ALSO FOR PRACTICE

Who do we research for, and who is the audience of our research? How can we involve stakeholders in our efforts? There have been various suggestions and initiatives to include stakeholders other than just ourselves (Aguinis et al., 2014). It is not a new observation that there is a wide gap between research and practice in management research. The causes of and potential solutions to this gap have been widely debated for a long time (Rynes, Bartunek, and Daft, 2001). This has been a core issue raised by many scholars, journal editors, and various organizational initiatives, such as those set up by RRBM and the AOM Practice Theme Committee.

We need to extend our knowledge about a phenomenon in order to intensify our interactions with that phenomenon. For example, Starkey et al. (2009: 557) suggest that we create a research process that is framed in terms of shared meaning that aligns researchers, research users, and the stakeholder community. We may in that way identify vocabularies and methodologies that lead to more effective management regimes. Bartunek (2007) suggests closer relations between academics and practitioners—beyond research collaborations. Rousseau's (2006) AOM presidential address in 2005 has been widely cited. In her opinion, evidence-based management provides the model needed to close the research–practice gap.

Journals and Editors: Forums or Special Issues

In recent years, journals and journal editors have raised concern regarding the lack of stakeholder inclusion in management journals and publications. The number of forums and special issues on academic–practitioner relations has exploded since the turn of the millennium (Bartunek and Rynes, 2014), including issues of the *Academy of Management Journal* (2001), *British Journal of Management* (2001), *European Management Journal* (2002), *Human Resource Management* (2004), *Journal of Management Studies* (2009), *Journal of Management Inquiry* (2009), *Organization Studies* (2010), *Journal of Applied Behavioral Science* (2011), *Journal of Business and Psychology* (2011), *Academy of Management Perspectives* (2012), *Journal of Management* (2014), *Journal of Business Economics* (2014), *Academy of Management Learning and Education* (2014), and so forth.

As early as 2001, *Academy of Management Journal* (AMJ) published a special issue on closing the research–practitioner gap (Rynes, Bartunek, and Daft, 2001). This was also the background for the *British Journal of Management* (BJM) special issue in 2001, about realigning stakeholders in management research (Hodgkinson, Herriot, and Anderson, 2001). An important part of the discussion here was that relevance and rigor were not balanced, and that rigor had outcompeted relevance. The 2009 special issue of the *Journal of Management Studies* (JMS) on management research updated many of the debates rehearsed in the 2001 BJM special issue. In the JMS special issue, Starkey, Hatchuel, and Tempest (2009) showed that the present trend of giving primacy to the pursuit of rigor deemphasized the importance of relevance, and argued that we should realign relevance as a necessary condition for rigor. This should lead to new forms of engagement with theory and practice. The JMS special issue showed a new concern for holism and sensitivity to action, dynamics, context, and complexity. A main argument related to showing that it is possible to temper deductive ambition and encourage inductive thinking and research practice. The *Journal of Management* had a special issue in 2014 on the academic–practitioner gap (Bartunek and Rynes, 2014).

RRBM[3]

RRBM is a virtual organization (Tsui, 2018). It was founded by leading business scholars across five disciplines and from a large number of university-based business schools in ten countries. It was later joined by a growing community of scholars from all over the worlds. RRBM is supported by many partners, including accreditation organizations such as AACSB and EFMD. Its objective is to ensure responsible research with the production of credible knowledge that can be used to inform progressive government policies and promote positive business and management practices. RRBM calls for actions to transform business and management research toward achieving a better world.

RRBM has a vision (Vision 2030) that business schools worldwide should be admired for their contribution to societal wellbeing (Tsui, 2018), and to support this journey RRBM suggests seven principles to guide responsible research. These relate to service to society, stakeholder involvement, impact on stakeholders, basic and implied contributions, plurality and multidisciplinarity, sound methodology, and broad dissemination. Four of them focus primarily on the usefulness of knowledge and three on the credibility of knowledge.

RRBM calls for a change to the research ecosystem. RRBM claims that acting on the seven principles of responsible research requires a revision of criteria, processes, and incentive systems at all levels: individual faculty, journals, and schools. However, it is not sufficient for RRBM to proclaim principles. There is also a need to modify the ecosystem of research so that individual researchers are rewarded for making progress toward the achievement of our higher goals.

RRBM reclaims the need for a scholarly identity, which it sees as involving the search for knowledge and discovery as well as a focus on impacts on both science and policy/practice. This is more important than the "getting a paper published" identity. The scholarly identity should recognize multiple forms of producing and disseminating knowledge.

RRBM argues for a publishing and reward system that goes beyond theoretical gap spotting. We as scholars should train ourselves and our doctoral students to speak to practitioners. To fulfill Vision 2030 and to pursue responsible research, RRBM argues, synchronized action is

---

[3]   RRBM and the audience, https://www.rrbm.network/ accessed September 17, 2019.

required across all relevant stakeholder groups, with the common goal of valuing rigorous scholarship that will result in actionable knowledge. RRBM suggests possible actions by key stakeholders such as journal editors and publishers, scholarly association leaders, university leaders, deans and senior scholars, business school associations, accrediting and ranking agencies, funding agencies and governments, scholars, other external stakeholders, and coordinated commitment mechanisms.

AOM Practice Theme

The assessment of scholarly impact, coupled with growing concern over the diminished relevance of management scholarship to practice, has assumed great importance and relevance for all AOM members. Thus a workforce established by the AOM Practice Theme Committee conducted an all-Academy study to identify resources in which the AOM may invest to address members' research, teaching, and training needs to achieve scholarly impact.[4] The AOM Practice Theme workforce concluded with the following suggestions: "Broaden measures of scholarly impact, broaden participation, increase assessment weights for practical impacts in journals, invest in translating research for dissemination, initiate consortia with other academies, build impact evaluation groups, change reward structures, provide mentoring."

MESSAGE—FROM GETTING PUBLISHED TO MEANINGFUL RESEARCH

Reshaping Relevance and Impact

How can we conduct impactful management research? For whom and when is impactful management research created? MacIntosh et al. (2017) addressed this as the editors of a special issue of BJM in 2017. They elaborated four ideal types of impact by articulating both the constituencies for whom impact occurs and the form it may take. They suggested that management as a discipline would benefit when practice, research, and scholarship are more intertwined.

Several scholars have led crusades against the lack of meaning in the POP culture. Some argue that a new science of management research is

---

[4]   AOM Practice Theme 2018.

needed (Starkey et al., 2009). Pettigrew and Alvesson argue in various contributions that we need to rethink our professional norms, and to cultivate a more scholarly identity. Through a long series of publications, they have raised concerns regarding the management profession, and that we as management scholars are meeting neither rigor nor relevance criteria. They focus on the need for meaningful, reflective, and impactful research. They have also discussed the future of business schools.

Glynn, as outgoing AOM president, argued that fundamental changes are needed to support and applaud scholarly research (Glynn, 2019). She argued that our research should contribute to social welfare. McGahan (2018) was even more direct in her presidential address:

> We should free ourselves to work only on things that are important in the world and have meaning for ourselves personally. We should make sure that we at the end of our careers, we can look back with satisfaction that we have been standing up against suffering, inequality, and impoverishment; that we have been standing up for freedom, sustainability and creativity; that we have used the prosperity we enjoy to make the world better. (2018: 175)

Grand Challenges

It has been suggested that our research should address the great challenges in society (for example Eisenhardt, Graebner, and Sonenshein, 2016; George et al., 2016; Levin et al., 2012). This is, as previously indicated, in alignment with several of the addresses given by the outgoing AOM presidents, and EURAM's grand challenges agenda (see Chapters 3 and 4).

Grand challenges include existential risks—risks that could end humanity, such as nuclear catastrophes resulting from accidents or war; climate change and the destruction of the natural environment; and unintended consequences of artificial intelligence. However, they also include challenges such as inequality, poverty, ecological imbalances, and socioeconomic and political crises. The United Nations' Sustainability Agenda has been developed to transform the world with this in mind.[5]

We can approach the grand challenges through considering new and interesting avenues for research, but also through making them the core of why we do research. The existential risks facing humanity require

---

[5]　www.un.org/sustainabledevelopment/development-agenda/　accessed September 17, 2019.

knowledge not just of how to manage within an organization, but also how to design and manage the relationships between them to avoid, on a global scale, the tragedy of the commons. Research related to the grand challenges may require alternative and innovative methods and ways of communication, including for example inductive methods (Eisenhardt et al., 2016) and action research (Ferraro, Etzion, and Gehman, 2015). George et al. (2016) developed, through a special issue in AMJ, a framework to guide future research in formulating, articulating, and implementing research about grand challenges. They challenge researchers to engage in collaborative endeavors to tackle these issues.

I coorganized a symposium on existential risks at the EURAM meeting in 2019. In this symposium, we discussed how extending management education into this dimension would mean introducing some fundamental changes. Furthermore, physical metrics of the wellbeing of the environment and humans would need to replace undefinable social constructs such as economic value or costs. Empirical research and/or case studies based on increasing profits in the private sector or reducing costs in the nonprofit and government sectors could be counterproductive. A mission statement for management education expanded to sustain humanity could be "To acquire and share knowledge for managing human wellbeing for eternity."[6]

As indicated in the previous chapter, EURAM has decided that all symposium proposals for their upcoming conferences need to be related to some of the United Nations sustainability goals.

Returning to Meaning and Polymorphic Research

Mats Alvesson's is one of the strongest critical voices against the present POP culture, and he calls for meaningful research. Alvesson et al. (2017) critically describe the present publishing culture. They make distinctions among problem definitions and solutions at individual, institutional, and policy levels. They do not present one main solution or one way of solving everything, but they rather offer many small messages that they argue can contribute to give meaning. Their first suggestion is "reorientation of social science research from the omnipresent requirement to continuously publish in highly ranked journals to the overriding goal and

---

[6]   Presentation by Shann Turnbull at the EURAM 2019 symposium on existential risk.

purpose of creating original knowledge that matters to society" (2017: 85).

Alvesson and Gabriel (2013) criticize the strong conformist tendency in research. Research criteria and ideals that may be reasonable and convenient for some types of research can be harmful when adopted uncritically across the board. They argue that our research is too focused on gap spotting. Instead, it should be path setting. They argue for polymorphic research, less formulaic research, and a nomadic research trajectory.

Openness and curiosity are key virtues in polymorphic research. The point of polymorphism, according to Alvesson and Gabriel, is to open up alternative ways of thinking and writing research. Polymorphic research acknowledges uncertainties and doubts, has a method based on reflexivity, aims at nonstandardized text production, and addresses a broad audience. The authors argue that it is vital for the academic community to work in a variety of ways to develop good scholarship, including developing innovative ideas, practicing reflexivity and writing creatively (2013: 256).

CHANNELS—THE METRICS BEING USED BEYOND PUBLISHING IN PRESTIGIOUS JOURNALS

How do we measure scholarly impact (Aguinis et al., 2014)? The use of impact assessments can bring many benefits. However, there are many unintended consequences that may be harming scholarship and creating flaws in the system. Scholarly associations, for example, have taken initiatives against journal ranking systems. In Britain around 2010, diverging lines of interest arose about journal rankings between the business schools (Association of Business Schools, ABS) and the leadership of the British Academy of Management (BAM).

One line of the channel discussion relates to metrics and academic ranking, and how this ranking system can lead to scientific misconduct. Among the most powerful initiatives to change the metrics have come from DORA and Anne-Wil Harzing.

DORA—The San Francisco Declaration[7]

The San Francisco Declaration, also called DORA (Declaration of Research Assessment), highlights the problems arising due to the focus on journal metrics and shows possible directions that may be taken by all stakeholders involved in evaluating academic research and scholarships. This declaration addresses research and sciences in general, not only management research. DORA has been signed by about 15,000 individuals and about 1000 organizations. All DORA signatories have, at a minimum, committed not to use journal-based metrics as an indicator for measuring the quality of individual research articles, to assess an individual scholar's contributions, or in hiring, promoting, or funding research decisions. Journal impact factor (JIF) is one such metric. This may have implications for the choice and use of journal lists.

DORA's ambition is to change practice in research assessment, which involves changing the academic culture and behavior to ensure that hiring, promotion, and funding decisions focus on the qualities of the research. DORA focuses on insight, impact, reliability, and reusability rather than what it calls questionable proxies. The DORA guidance includes approaching funding agencies and institutions, publishers, metrics providers, and researchers. DORA emphasizes the importance of exploring new approaches to assessment, and with greater transparency around the effectiveness of these approaches, improvements will spread more rapidly. For the purposes of research assessment, the value and impact of all research outputs should be considered. That goes beyond publications, including a broad range of impact measures as qualitative indicators of research impact, such as influence on policy and practice.

As mentioned earlier, I have signed the DORA declaration. I then committed to challenge research assessment practices that rely inappropriately on JIF. I have also committed to talk to colleagues and to advocate for change. As an author, reviewer, or editor I shall not support journals that use JIF as a marketing tool or any request to consider journal metrics in decisions on manuscripts.

However, getting signatories to the declaration is just the first step toward changing practice in research assessment for DORA, especially considering how deeply rooted journal metrics have become. DORA was established to help the community move forward, and a DORA roadmap

---

[7]   The presentation of DORA is based on extracts from https://sfdora.org/.

was published in 2018. The roadmap emphasizes that after signing: "The next and more challenging steps for signatories require changes in academic culture and behavior to ensure that hiring, promotion, and funding decisions focus on the qualities of research that are most desirable—insight, impact, reliability and reusability—rather than on questionable proxies."

DORA promotes the adoption of the Contributor Role Taxonomy (CRediT), to more clearly identify and recognize the work of each author,[8] to promote the use of ORCID IDs,[9] and to support the Initiative for Open Citations I4OC.[10]

DORA is addressing the challenges on a global scale, and seeks to establish globally supportive communities. However, there is no one size fits all solution, and DORA is thus stimulating the signatories to be leaders—to talk to colleagues and advocate for change.

Beyond Traditional Metrics

Anne-Wil Harzing has a reputation for offering new ways in which bibliometrics can be used to assess academic performance. This includes the development of her Publish or Perish software system.[11] Through several contributions (for example Adler and Harzing, 2009), she has demonstrated the problems of the present dominant JIF ranking system. Her criticism of JIF has facilitated the use of a large number of alternative or supplementary metrics. Harzing's software system retrieves and analyzes academic citations, and it uses Google Scholar to obtain the raw citations.

Adler and Harzing (2009) position a discussion of research metrics in the question of what our research is actually contributing. In past decades, the use of metrics for research evaluation has become an integral part of the academic landscape. However, Adler and Harzing argue that since the reversal of this trend is unlikely, research into fairer and more inclusive ways of measuring research performance is gaining more and more momentum.

Adler and Harzing (2009) show that current ranking systems are dysfunctional and potentially cause more harm than good. They show the

---

[8]   See for example www.casrai.org/credit.html.
[9]   See for example https://orcid.org/.
[10]   See for example https://i4oc.org/.
[11]   https://harzing.com/resources/publish-or-perish accessed September 17, 2019.

arbitrary nature of JIF as a ranking system, and they invite the worldwide community of scholars to innovate and design more reliable and valid ways to assess scholarly contributions. They raise critical questions about which publications are included in JIF, and they argue that the type of publications included need to become more global and comprehensive. They ask questions about why only articles are important, why only in the English language, and why international scholarship is viewed below domestic scholarship. They argue that journals fail as proxies for quality, and that being more prolific does not guarantee impact.

To solve these problems Adler and Harzing call for an immediate examination of existing ranking systems. This should not only be done as a legitimate scholarly question vis-á-vis performance or through a conceptual lens with deep roots in management research. It is urgent because the very health and vibrancy of our scholarly society are at stake. Adler and Harzing

> suggest to institute a temporary moratorium on institutional rankings, better understand and subsequently address the macro level dynamics that collude in keeping such dysfunctional system in place, design individual rankings, and to create an environment that form and appreciate excellence in scholarship on the questions that matter most to business and society. (Adler and Harzing, 2009: 84)

Adler and Harzing conclude in their study of metrics that the key question is always: "Has the scholar asked an important question and investigated it in such a way that it has the potential to advance societal understanding and well-being?" (2009: 92) However, rather than allowing assessment and ranking systems to continue to consume disproportionate amounts of universities' attention and resources, academia needs to shift to designing and implementing environments that purposefully encourage research that matters.

COMMUNITY—FROM EGOCENTRICITY TO A SHARING PHILOSOPHY

AOM Presidents and EURAM

In Chapter 3, the arguments and reflections of outgoing AOM presidents were summarized in eight points: the role of scholars, dysfunctional metrics, lack of relevance, institutional pressures, reframing international dialogues, creating a sustainable community of scholars, the importance of compassion, and research for the future. Many of the concerns of these former AOM presidents are reflected in the above presented initiatives. However, the importance of our academic community is emphasized in most of the AOM presidential addresses. They argue that we should be a vibrant and engaged community. We should care about each other, and senior scholars should support their more junior colleagues. We should believe in the training of teachers. A major issue is developing a community that enables collective action and change—a community that is educating hearts. Similar reflections were presented in Chapter 4 on EURAM.

Creating a New Game—Not Only Isomorphism

In the coming chapters I will present aspects of a sharing philosophy in research. The sharing philosophy is communal, open, and impact-driven. The Norefjell clan is in Chapter 6 illustrating the communal approach. Norefjell is a skiing resort in Norway, and a community, programmatic research, and a distinct research stream were developed through the annual workshops there. An open and holistic approach to research is illustrated in Chapter 7 through the small, private Witten/Herdecke University in Germany. This university is rooted in an anthroposophical philosophy focused on the integration of head, heart, and hands as well as the importance of passion and compassion. The importance of working with young scholars and their development is emphasized in this chapter, including the focus on second and third order effects of our scholarly activities. Chapter 8 uses the Women on Boards Cruise Workshops to illustrate the importance of societal impact and contributions, and how our research community should be directed towards the welfare and wellbeing of the world. Venturesome avenues for conducting impactful research are presented in this chapter. Polymorphic research is presented in the chapter as an important concept that can help direct our research to relevance and meaning.

Is this a new game in doing research? Or is this a return to the past—a past of true scholarship? This is not isomorphism or simply an adjustment of the existing game; it is a rethinking of our professional norms.

PART II

A sharing philosophy

6.   A communal approach—the clan

CREATING COMMUNITIES OF SCHOLARS

My understanding about doing international research has been deeply changing
after my first experience at the Norefjell workshop. Being a part of an international community on a specific topic is more than writing, with other international colleagues, academic papers that can be published in the top journals.
Being part of an international community means consolidating together shared
values and convergent believes; it means discussing and sharing ideas about the
development of the field, about contributions, about impactful research. The
Norefjell workshop has the power of giving you the idea that all together we
can really contribute and inspire other people, doing meaningful research. The
Norefjell workshop is the place in which new collaborations start. It is the place
in which new long-term projects begins. But what is even more important, it is the common values that we build and we share that let to this international community to inspire the society with a common language and message,
and contribute to the development of it. (Alessandra Rigolini, 2019)[1]

Many of my PhD students have come to me telling me that they want to
work as consultants. I am happy to hear that, and I was myself a management consultant before I started my PhD track. However, I also reveal to
them that I would like to see them take some additional steps. I would
like them to be the consultants of consultants, or even the consultants of
the consultants' consultants. I want the students to become the teachers
of teachers, the professors of professors, or the mentors of mentors.
Through these reflections, we can see what is meant by the second and
third order impact that should characterize the ERC criteria of excellence
in scholarship.

Building communities of engaged scholars and creating a vibrant
community are challenges we met in Chapter 3 on the Academy of
Management (AOM) and in Chapter 4 on the European Academy of
Management (EURAM). Here I present the example, and my experi-

---

[1]   Alessandra Rigolini is an associate professor at the University of Pisa. She
is among those who initiated Norefjell events after I decided to retire.

ences, of building the Norefjell "clan." The Norefjell "clan" is the result of a communal approach, including communal and joint credit and giving credit for research and not only publications. It is about creating communities of engaged scholars.

UNDERSTANDING ACTUAL BOARD BEHAVIOR— THE HUMAN SIDE OF BOARDS, GOVERNANCE, AND VALUE CREATION

Developing a Language

When I present myself, I often communicate that I am a concept-developing researcher, doing programmatic research. My objective is to contribute to developing a language to help us understand boards of directors, and my "hobby" is to develop and use a variety of methods to respond to my research agenda.

The majority of my research has focused on studies of boards of directors. When starting a presentation or a speech for business people or PhD students on this topic, I like to have a glass of wine in my hand. I use the glass of wine to reflect on concepts. Research about boards and corporate governance usually leans on a handful of main concepts, and these concepts help us understand the field. The most used concepts are board size, insider–outsider ratio, CEO duality, and the board members' shareholding. Nuances around these four concepts are supposed to explain most of the variations in corporate financial performance. I argue that we need a much bigger dictionary or toolbox.

First, I make the audience see that their wine-related vocabulary is much bigger than five words. I show them that despite their awareness of many technical words and phrases—red versus white wine, still or sparkling, grape variations, country of production and price—they can still learn much about wine. Second, I often tell them that my favorite grape is pinot noir, and the best wine I drink may be an old Bordeaux wine (not pinot noir grape), but my best wine experiences depend on my mood and the people I am together with. Most often I then drink something other than a pinot noir or an old Bordeaux. Through my glass of wine, I communicate the importance of developing a language about boards and corporate governance.

We see and experience through the concepts we know. They are our spectacles, and the concepts fill our dictionary or the toolkit with which we make sentences, make equations, and propose ways to improve boards and business performance. I use my concepts to tell a story about boards of directors with a focus on actual behavior, understanding people and even our own feelings.

A Long-Term Research Agenda on Actual Board Behavior[2]

I have studied boards of directors for many years, and my research has gone hand in hand with my experiences as a board member in several types of organizations. In 1989, when I decided to study for a PhD, it was not difficult to choose to study topics around boards of directors. In the immediate years before starting my PhD work, I was a consultant with a focus on training and recruiting board members. I was involved in developing boards and training board members. As I returned to academia in 1989, I needed to update my knowledge and to learn about new developments in board literature. I had to learn about agency theory, and I visited scholars that seemed to be important for developing the research area of boards of directors. During January and February 1990, I thus traveled to meet some of those that I discovered were among the most outstanding scholars influencing my interest about boards.

At Harvard Business School, I met with world leading scholars such as Miles Mace, Kenneth Andrews, Michael Porter, Michael Ruback, and Jay Lorsch. All openly and extensively shared their experiences. The meeting with Miles Mace was probably the peak of the Harvard experience. He had retired and was already blind at that time, and he came to his office at Harvard just to meet me. He repeatedly told me of the gap between myths and realities, and that we need to understand the reasons behind this gap. We need to understand the power dynamics, decision structures, and identities of the board members. We need to understand the real game.

At Wharton and at Texas A&M I was also received by several outstanding scholars, including Peter Lorange, Don Hellriegel, Jay Barney, and Barry Baysinger. Don Hellriegel was amazingly supportive and accommodating, and I highly appreciated the conceptual clarity about boards that Barry Baysinger introduced to me. I also met with some impressive junior scholars during the US trip, including Rita Kosnik and Idie Kesner. They shared their reflections about publishing and doing research on boards of directors.

---

2   This paragraph builds on and reflects Huse (2008b).

Rita and Idie came from different research traditions, but both of them wanted me to pay attention to a young scholar that just had published a review paper in *Journal of Management*. This young and unestablished scholar was Shaker Zahra. Over the coming 20 years I spent considerable time with Shaker, and we became close friends. He included me in his experiences and reflections on making an academic career, on academia, journals, research agendas, publishing techniques, and so forth. My approach to studying boards of directors thus was heavily influenced by him. He was also the one to introduce me to the dynamics at the AOM annual conferences.

A Stream of Research Is Developing

In the 1990s, I conducted a large number of studies of boards of directors. Some of these studies are presented and summarized in Huse (2008c).[3] I had started to study a phenomenon, and I applied different methods and theories in my attempts to understand the behavioral perspectives of boards of directors. However, most of the studies were close to practice, and I summarized my experiences and findings in developing research models containing testable hypotheses.

Toward the end of the 1990s, I was invited by Hans Landström to join him as an adjunct professor at Lund University and Halmstad University. My main position was then at the Centre for Church Research in Oslo. Together with Hans, we focused on boards and governance in entrepreneurial firms. Hans had a particular passion for exploring and understanding research streams, and I joined him in some of his efforts to explore variations among research streams in entrepreneurship research. In the Lund/Halmstad period, we started organizing international PhD workshops on governance in SMEs.

I remember this period with a warm feeling. There were two publications resulting from the courses, which described the content, lecturers, and literature, as well as selected papers. From a citation point of view, the pub-lications have zero value, but for many who participated in the course—me included—they had an impact. The publications created meaning and a sense of belongingness, and together with the PhD courses, they connected young European scholars with an interest in boards and governance. Several of us

---

[3]   Chapter 10 in Huse (2008c) is about methods and concepts in studies about value-creating boards. Some of my studies from the 1990s are presented in this anthology.

have stayed connected in different ways during our scholarly careers. (Jonas Gabrielsson, 2019[4])

In this period, together with Jonas Gabrielsson, one of my students at that time, I continued developing largescale questionnaire surveys about actual board behavior in Swedish firms. The survey instrument was a follow-up of my previous board studies (for summaries see Huse, 1995; 2007), and directly led to the value-creating board survey instrument (Huse, 2008d).

The Value-Creating Board Survey Instrument

The first version of the value-creating board framework was presented in 2002, and we got a large research grant that became the starting point for the Value Creating Board Research Program at BI Norwegian Business School.[5] The framework was used to develop the value-creating board research project as well as the value-creating board survey instrument. After several pilot studies, the first version of the instrument was launched during the fall of 2003. Scholars from various European countries came together in winter 2004 to explore how this instrument could be scrutinized also outside Norway. We met in Oslo and at Norefjell.

The value-creating board survey instrument exists in two main editions, and has been used in various countries. The second edition was developed based on lessons from the first edition. General scales were then changed from five points to seven points, and items and variables were revised after detailed empirical validation through the first edition. Versions of the first edition have been used in the Netherlands, Belgium, Italy, and Norway. Versions of the second edition have been used in Norway, Turkey, Denmark, and Finland. Versions of the instrument have also been used in other countries as its design and questions have been made openly available to scholars in general. The survey instruments and data from the two main versions are now openly available at BI's Research Depository (BIRD).

---

[4]　Jonas Gabrielsson is Professor and Dean of School of Business and Technology at Halmstad University.

[5]　In 2002, BI was called Norwegian School of Management BI.

THE NOREFJELL COMMUNITY

The Norefjell Board Governance Research Workshops

The Norefjell Board Governance International Research Workshops on Behavioural Perspectives of Boards (Norefjell workshops)[6] have been organized every year since the spring 2004. The workshop started as a meeting place for scholars wanting to explore and work together on the value-creating board survey instrument. The Norefjell workshops were mostly held at the same mountain lodge at Norefjell, but in some years were organized elsewhere. Norefjell is a skiing resort two hours' drive away from Oslo. In 1952, Norefjell was the venue for downhill competitions at the Olympic Games.

At the Norefjell workshops, all participants lived together for three to four days. The participants were mostly PhD students and junior faculty, and they stayed together, mostly in one main living room, for academic work, social activities and skiing, and practical activities, including meals and meal preparation. There were plenary discussions, group discussions, and paper presentations. On average, about 25 PhD students and faculty attended each year. The attendees came from a large number of countries. In total, there have been more than 100 separate participants at the workshops.

In the beginning, the workshops were directly linked to the Value Creating Board Research Program at BI Norwegian Business School. The scope increased as this research program ended, and alternative ways of exploring actual board behavior and behavioral perspectives of boards and governance got more space. Sponsors from business were recruited, and these sponsors attended the workshops. Board Governance, a Denmark-based organization training boards and board members, was the main sponsor for several years.

Before the 2017 workshop, I decided to reduce my involvement and opened space for initiatives by others.[7]

---

[6]   This was the formal name for several years. Board Governance is the name of a main sponsor of the workshops.

[7]   I decided to reduce my involvement as I was planning my retirement. Since 2018, others have organized "Norefjell workshops."

The Norefjell "Clan"—A Communal Approach

"Norefjell clan" is a term used by some of the regular participants at the annual Norefjell research workshops. It is used to show their identification with the group, mostly socially, but also academically. "Norefjell group" or "community" are terms used more broadly about the workshop participants. At Norefjell, the junior participants had opportunities to meet with senior scholars, fellowshipping, presenting, and getting comments on their work in progress, listening to presentations about behavioral perspectives and boards, and being mentored. A strong social cohesiveness developed among the participants. There was no social hierarchy at the workshops and the participants were generally in a mood of open sharing with each other. Many of the participants found new research partners, publication partners, and consulting partners during the workshops.

There was a sharing philosophy behind the workshops, including sharing of ideas, sharing of data, and sharing of publications. We also shared wine, a kitchen, and sleeping space. During these workshops, we discussed and explored ways to research and understand the behavioral perspectives of boards of directors. These workshops were the cornerstone of development of a distinct international research stream about boards of directors. A core contribution from the Norefjell workshops was developing and nurturing the scholarly identity of researchers. There was a social purpose: care for the participants, including teaching and education through sharing, supporting, and mentoring—balancing their short-term and long-term requirements. The overall, long-term objective was to make research more impactful through second and third-order effects, like nuclear processes linking atoms to research and research dissemination—with consequences for theory and practice.

The Norefjell community can be characterized as a virtual organization. It is a vibrant community where a joint language about boards and governance has evolved. Knowledge about boards of directors and research about boards of directors developed together. In the Norefjell community, there was a focus on value-creating boards and behavioral perspectives, but not a strong emphasis on detailed findings and knowledge within a narrowly defined field. There was a call for responsible science, and the promotion of transparency, open sharing, and reproducibility. The purpose was not to find a final truth, but rather to challenge, commenting on and finding alternatives to existing knowledge. The Norefjell community was the result of a communal approach, including communal and joint credit—giving credit for research and not only for publications. It was about creating communities of engaged scholars.

Norefjell and EURAM

There are links between the Norefjell community and EURAM. At the EURAM conference that took place in Stockholm in 2002, Jonas Gabrielsson and I organized a track on boards and corporate governance. About 20 different papers were presented, and some of the contributors were about to commence similar work to mine and Jonas'. During the EURAM and EGOS meetings in 2003, we continued organizing various activities. We also invited some of the EURAM and EGOS participants to develop, together with us, international versions of the value-creating board survey instrument. As mentioned earlier, during winter 2004 we met in Oslo, and the first Norefjell workshop was held.

During the Norefjell workshops, we discussed group meeting places in addition to Norefjell. We found that coming together once a year was not enough to develop a community. We thus considered meeting during the EGOS meetings, during the EURAM meetings, or during the AOM meetings. We found the EURAM meetings to be the most feasible. Here it was most certain that we could permanently organize our tracks about boards and corporate governance. The Norefjell community thus found EURAM as a second home, and when strategic interest groups (SIGs) were formalized in EURAM in 2009, the corporate governance group already had its core membership. The corporate governance SIG later became the mother of several of the other SIGs. Many from the Norefjell clan later served as officers in the EURAM corporate governance SIG, and some have even been presidents or vice-presidents of EURAM.

Another question discussed related to publishing and journals. Typically, many in the Norefjell group submitted their paper proposals to EURAM, but also to AOM and EGOS. But what about journals? I had felt when publishing that I should see my publication as a contribution in a conversation with an audience, and thus I preferred special rather than general journals. As a matter of principle, I also wanted to support the development of European or international journals. Most of the leading general journals in management leaned very heavily on US-based editorships, research questions, and empirical data (Gabrielsson and Huse, 2004). Even the citations followed an American pattern: reference should preferably be made to a few accepted journals, and to English-language contributions only.

Some journals became particularly valuable to the Norefjell community. For some years, I had been on the editorial board of the *Journal of Management and Governance* (JMG), and its editor, Anna Grandori, had attended a Norefjell workshop. JMG thus became an important publication alternative. Three other journals also became important as clan outlets. These were *Corporate Governance: An International Review* (CGIR), *International Journal of Business Governance and Ethics* (IJBGE), and *European Management Review* (EMR): EMR because it was the journal of EURAM, IJBGE because of its focus and the fact one of the Norefjell community was its editor, and CGIR because it was in the process of becoming more scientific and several of us became involved in its editorship.

PROGRAMMATIC RESEARCH AND A DISTINCT RESEARCH STREAM ABOUT VALUE-CREATING BOARDS

Programmatic Research

Lee (2009) and DeNisi (2010) argued in their AOM presidential addresses for programmatic research. The Norefjell story is about programmatic research. In his AOM presidential address, Lee (2009:197) argued: "When I think about our academic research, it's been my experience that one publication seldom has a large influence on our theory and research. Instead, it is a stream of programmatic research involving many different kinds of books, articles, and chapters that deeply affects our thinking and actions."

> First, we should be less concerned about the contribution of individual studies and more concerned about the contribution of programmatic bodies of research. Further, I believe that such programmatic research should be our gold standard for meaningful academic scholarship. Second, most contemporary research issues and the everyday constraints imposed by a business school require a diverse skill set and multiple points of view for programmatic scholarship, particularly in today's global marketplace for research and publication. In other words, I believe that team-based research is the most effective strategy to conduct programmatic scholarship in today's environment. (2009: 197–8)

DeNisi followed up the year after by arguing: "we really need to look at research programs and streams rather than individual studies ...

therefore, perhaps we should be encouraging young scholars to develop coherent research programs, rather than rewarding them for publishing the 'five required A-level articles' necessary for tenure" (2010: 195).

Following Lee and DeNisi, programmatic research is a set of studies around a common theme, examining, describing and addressing a fundamental or challenging issue, problem, phenomena, or outcome. It comprises a range of themes which are coherent and aligned, and allow comprehensive breadth of analytical foci, research outcomes, and findings. Lee illustrated programmatic research through his experiences with colleagues in exploring why people stay in their jobs. DeNisi used the work of the Nobel Prize winner Daniel Kahneman to show the importance of programmatic research.

In programmatic research, it is important to lean on a strong paradigm, but it involves strong team synergies to facilitate shared expertise, knowledge exchange, and collaboration. It involves investing in people. Programmatic research may incorporate multilevel, multimethod, multiperspective, and multidisciplinary approaches. Several bias problems in research are thus reduced, including common method bias problems. Programmatic research will have strong translational efforts as a part of its agenda, including encouraging stakeholders to be actively involved.

> The focus on single papers and their citations is too atomistic, and does not make much sense when you think about the broader meaning of scholarly work and writing as engaging in conversations. When belonging to a programmatic research stream my research gets a value and meaning beyond the contribution of paper A and paper B, which jointly may be important carriers of meaning together with other contributions in a system of understanding of a common theme. This way of seeing research is poetry for scholars. (Jonas Gabrielsson, 2019)

Continuity of research is important. The principles and facts of developmental guidance and counseling require research that is longitudinal. Even short-term problem-solving counseling often depends upon personal history data and, therefore, also upon long-term research. These are features of programmatic research. Being involved in a programmatic line of research on one topic may help young scholars in their transition to becoming experienced and successful scholars. This is what we experienced during the Norefjell workshops and in the Norefjell community.

Programmatic Research about Value-Creating Boards

Figure 6.1 displays research developed around the Norefjell workshops. Business case studies of boards were the starting point for the workshops, for the value-creating board framework, and for the survey instrument. The business case studies were developed in depth through the inclusion of new analyses, new variables, new surveys, and alternative methods, and with research from various contextual settings, including countries. Some of the new variables and analyses included were related to women on boards.

Additional questions developed about behavioral perspectives of boards developed. While the business case studies had a meso- or board-level focus, we then also included more studies on the micro level—understanding individual board members, who they are, and their behavior. We also studied the women becoming board members, the main actors involved in the discussions about getting women on boards, and the interactions between the two. On the other side, we started to include more macro-level studies. We tried to include issues we saw as important for the future development of boards, corporations, and society, and we made explorations going beyond Norway, Europe, and the western world. We started to ask questions about the value-creating role of boards in other cultures, for example India and the Arab Middle

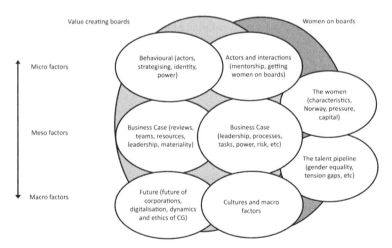

Figure 6.1   *Programmatic research: studying a phenomenon and research streams*

East. In addition, we started inquiring about the future of corporations, corporate governance, and boards.

Our programmatic research did not stop there. A new agenda was about to develop: that of getting women on boards. This agenda, and lessons from it, is presented in Chapter 8. The focus then moved from the business case and the value-creating board to questions about societal value creation, equality, sustainability, and wellbeing.

A Distinct Research Stream

The value-creating board research from the Norefjell group constitutes a distinct research stream. This can be observed in bibliometric analyses, such as that by Zheng and Kouwenberg (2019). Zheng and Kouwenberg show through a cocitation mapping how my research on boards is tightly related to some of the other researchers attending the Norefjell workshop,[8] for example Alessandro Zattoni. Our work is close to the contributions of Shaker Zahra, Dan Forbes and Frances Milliken, Amy Hillman, and Andrew Pettigrew. Within the strategy and management fields, there are two other distinct streams. One is around Daily, Dalton, Johnson, and Ellstrand. The second is centered on Westphal, Hambrick, and Zajac. There are other streams about boards and corporate governance in fields such as law and accounting, finance, and economics.

What makes this research stream distinct? The value-creating board stream combines observations of actual board behavior with theoretical reflections, and is a result of an abductive approach. The cornerstones and building block were studied through several deductive as well as inductive projects about actual board behavior. The stream has links to US-based management strategy traditions with deductive approaches, as well as to European and Australian/New Zealand traditions that lean more on inductive approaches. A particular feature is the attention on processes and actual behavior used within the boardroom, and that board performance and effectiveness are measured in intermediate steps. "Value creation" refers to the board's role in value creation and not only in "value distribution". This also means contributions in innovation and entrepreneurial behavior.

---

[8]   Their study is based on Web of Science and Scopus data.

Most of the empirical studies have been performed in Europe with European data. This has also shaped the stream:

- First, in Europe there is an awareness of variations in corporate governance systems and board accountability.
- Second, within national European settings, most firms are considered as small or medium sized, compared to the Fortune 500 companies that are used in many US-based studies.
- Third, the tenure track system for faculty in Europe was not as developed during the 1980s–2000s as it was in the US. That made it possible to do research with longer time horizons and possibilities to collect primary data.
- Fourth, scholars in Europe relate to research and research traditions published in various languages and in other outlets than those common in the US. This may contribute to more venturesome and diverse research designs.

This stream brings together behavioral, institutional, entrepreneurial, and ethical approaches to the study of boards and governance. The research conducted spans legal and political debates on corporate governance from the macro to the micro level, and behavior inside and outside the boardroom. It relates to a variety of countries and contexts. There has been a core reasoning at the Norefjell workshops that research must be relevant and have an impact on business. The stream focuses on the importance of using behavioral perspectives, and that there are better ways of measuring processes than through proxies. Research has also been evaluated based on how it communicates with board members in small and medium sized companies.

A COMMUNAL APPROACH

A communal approach may be important in a sharing philosophy of research. In this chapter I have presented the background and development of the Norefjell community and its contribution to developing a research stream through a communal and programmatic research. The Norefjell workshops have called for responsible science, promoting transparency, open sharing, and reproducibility. The workshops have had a social purpose in caring for the participants, and a focus on second and third-order effects through teaching and educating the participants and through sharing, supporting, and mentoring.

> The Norefjell workshops have had a huge impact on my approach and thinking about research. The workshops have opened up doors to new concepts, and connected me to others who were working on similar things. However, most importantly, they gave a meaning to what I did and helped me to engage in conversations with others on things that we found interesting.
>
> In my view, the energy of the Norefjell workshops has been that people attending the workshops, scholars as well as practitioners, has been curious about and shared a similar interest in the behavioral dynamics of boards and governance. This curiosity has created an open atmosphere and a sharing attitude, where everyone contributes—and is allowed to contribute—with their points of view.
>
> The Norefjell workshops have created a unique scholarly conversation on the behavioral dynamics of boards and governance. A conversation lasts as long as people find it interesting to engage in it. It has no predetermined endpoint, and it is developing spontaneously in response to what has previously been said, sometimes in unpredictable ways. The Norefjell conversation has been going on since it started, and it continues to develop as oldtimers and newcomers come together to share their thoughts, ideas, and findings. To me, this represents the essence of engaged scholarship. (Jonas Gabrielsson, 2019)

7. An open innovation approach— head, heart, and hands

HOLISTIC AND PASSIONATE RESEARCH— EDUCATING THE HEART

In his benchmark contribution about true scholarship, Boyer (1990) argued that it is holistic, interdisciplinary, interpretive, and integrative. In their presidential speeches, some of the outgoing Academy of Management presidents highlighted the importance of educating the heart and not only the brain (Tung, 2005; Whetten, 2001), thinking and working holistically and multidisciplinary (Adler, 2016; McGahan, 2018), being passionate about our work (Smith, 2008), and passionately sharing our work with others (Glynn, 2019; Smith, 2008). We should do things we believe in (McGahan, 2018), and we should make our research and teaching contribute to changing lives (McGahan, 2018). We should make the world a better place to be (Cummings, 2007), and at the end of our careers we should be able to look back with satisfaction that we have stood up against suffering, inequality, and impoverishment and have improved the lives of people around us (McGahan, 2018).

We need to dare to care and even fight for what we believe in (Tung, 2005; von Glinow, 1996). Daring to care is crucial for the world (Tsui, 2013). Tsui (2013: 177) invited

> all to accept the compassion pledge by summoning the courage to conduct research that inspires managers to lead compassionately, to teach in ways that lead our students to act justly, to help our young colleagues make a difference, and to serve in ways that lead to a better Academy and a better world.

My 2012–17 late career experience from Witten/Herdecke University (UW/H) took me closer to many of these issues. This university, and my experiences there, became in some ways a philosophical lighthouse that helped me sort and navigate among many scholarly values. This is what I want to present in this chapter.

DeNisi (2011) challenged our scholarly practice by presenting the difference between the ideal scholarly community values and the dominating business community values. Science, and so academia, are seen as operating under a model of "the commons," where information is shared openly and ideas are discussed freely. In my Witten period, I experienced the importance of a community characterized by open sharing and open innovation.

EDUCATING TOMORROW'S THOUGHT LEADERS

The Education of the Next Generation of Thought Leaders?[1]

A few years ago I was asked to offer my reflections on what it will take to educate the next generations of thought leaders for a complicated world. My response was published in a booklet with a collection of other scholars' responses on the same question, and is as follows:

> I decided to spend some of my late career years at Witten/Herdecke University in Germany. This is the first private university in Germany, and it is based on anthroposophical values. The students are learning to use both brain and heart, and business disciplines are integrated with other disciplines, long term societal values are integrated with sustainable business values, and the teaching is based on discussions and reflection. I believe that this approach is important for educating generations of both business leaders and thought-leaders for a complicated world. This will also imply that we should educate our PhD students and new generations of scholars to value contributions and relevance at least as high as rigor. They must learn to believe in what they are doing in addition to learning the handicraft of publishing.
>
> There are needs for joint efforts among scholars to bypass the pressures for publications, and to focus on contributions. The present pressure in Europe to publish in certain journals will have a significant negative impact on doing meaningful research in a complicated world. Research needing innovative theories and methods, and based on local cultural heritage and empirical settings, are in the evolving publishing society discouraged. We need joint efforts in encouraging alternatives.

My period in Witten was important for focusing on true scholarly values, and for the development of my criticism of the present publish or perish culture. The Witten period also gave me many illustrations about exis-

---

[1] This paragraph follows what I wrote in Wright and Brown (2014).

tential research and that we in our research should address the grand challenges of our time. Some of them are presented below.

Existentialism and Great Challenges

Witten is a small town in the Ruhr area in Germany. It has about 100,000 inhabitants, but the whole Ruhr area has approximately six million people. Some of Witten's neighboring cities in the Ruhr area are Bochum, Dortmund, and Essen. Ruhr is famous for coal explorations and mining. It was in Witten that coal was first discovered, kicking off coal mining in the Ruhr area. The Ruhr area has been one of the main industrial regions in Europe, and during World War II it was extremely important for the German war machine. The Ruhr area became one of Europe's most important energy producing areas, but it also became one of the most polluted areas in Europe.

Because of its importance to the war, the area was heavily bombed. After the war, the region had to be rebuilt fast. Large numbers of guest workers and immigrants came to Ruhr to contribute to the rebuilding. These guest workers generally did not plan to remain in Germany, and typically sent their income back to their families in their home countries. However, many had children and then remained in Germany, though still with the idea that Germany was supposed to be a temporary place to stay. This had consequences for their children. The guest workers typically did not emphasize their children's education, and usually lacked ambitions for their future in Germany.

The Ruhr area has experienced grand challenges more than most other places in Europe, particularly on issues relating to pollution and immigration. Many of these challenges still exist, but the problems have been so visible and severe that they have formed politics and political decision makers—and also my reflections. The Ruhr area is today a green area, and people can go swimming in the beautiful Ruhr River. Highly polluting industries and energy providers have changed, and it has become one of Europe's most important showplaces for the transformation of energy production. Many of the issues that arose in relation to the guest workers have not been entirely addressed, but important ventures, for example in education, are now being implemented to meet them. For some time, the Ruhr area has needed to address some of the grand challenges of the present society, and I have seen that things need to be done and can be done.

Today, the metropolitan Ruhr, together with the Northern parts of the Rhine valley, is called the Los Angeles of Europe. This metropolitan area has about 12 million people. Most cities in this area can be reached within an hour's drive. Many of the top German football/soccer teams are from this area, many of the cities in this area have their own opera theaters and cultural attractions, and there are plenty of options for those enjoying shopping. The Ruhr metropolitan area is among the areas in Europe with the highest density of universities, research institutions, and cultural institutions. Its industrial and financial importance is also high. About one third of the largest companies on the German stock exchange (the DAX companies) have their head office here, and more than ten Fortune 500 companies have their head office in the region.

In my five-year period at UW/H, I regularly organized international PhD and junior faculty workshops, as well as events for business people. At most of these events I started by telling the story of Witten, the Ruhr area, and the grand challenges related to pollution and immigration, as well as the importance of doing existential research and teaching. We as scholars can and should have an impact on society. Scholarship is more than publishing and teaching from textbooks. We should educate the hearts of our students. We should educate tomorrow's thought leaders to have an impact on the transformation of society. We should not do this to get credit ourselves, but out of passion and a desire to contribute to the common good. This should also be the case when doing research following the United Nations sustainability goals.

Reflexive Thinking

One of my reasons for taking the late career position in Germany was the possibility to get to know and influence German gender equality politics, with a focus on getting a board gender quota regulation in Germany. I had already been included in such discussions in other countries, and some of my academic colleagues had invited me to advise politicians and bureaucrats in Germany. As part of this agenda, I was invited to become a member of the scientific advisory board of the Diversity Institute of Göttingen University in Germany. It has been a learning journey for me to be a member of this board. I became familiar with a reflexive research tradition (Alvesson and Sköldberg, 2017). Reflexivity in research refers to the circular relationship between cause and effect. It is an observer effect, and it includes a subjective process of self-consciousness.

Most of my research on diversity and gender equality has combined a positivistic-functional research tradition with a critical emancipating tradition. The first tradition generally uses a deductive research design, while the second uses inductive designs. At the research institute in Göttingen, I became curious about the reflexive research tradition, and I began to experiment with reflexive research. The reflexive tradition is different, not only because of its ontological background, but also in the topics being studied, the methods used, and its epistemological background. Abductive research designs were standard in this reflexive tradition. I was learning about ethnographic-inspired praxis theory and the role of systematic reflections on my background and experiences. This influenced me to develop a "champagne method" research design, which is presented in Chapter 8.

STANDING OUT—A LIGHTHOUSE: AN ALTERNATIVE STORY ABOUT A UNIVERSITY

The above heading was the title I used at a symposium presentation in 2017 at the European Academy of Management (EURAM) meeting in Glasgow. The title of the symposium was "Philosophy of management in practice: Knowledge, governance and legitimacy." I presented the philosophy I had explored during my 2012–17 professorship at UW/H. At the EURAM meeting two years previously, one of the presenters of a similar symposium listed some of the lighthouse universities in Europe. UW/H was one of them. I must admit that there was not always consistency between practice and the underlying philosophy at UW/H. The philosophy was not always an integrated part of the work of all my colleagues. Still, I saw the need for a university with such lighthouse values. I wanted UW/H to keep a position as a lighthouse that could help guide us to true scholarship.

In Glasgow, I presented the challenges in Witten and in the Ruhr area, and asked questions about what kinds of problems we face and what matters most. What kinds of business leaders do we want? How do we train our students? What kinds of universities do we want or need?

Witten/Herdecke University—Anthroposophy[2]

UW/H was established in 1982 and rooted in an anthroposophical/ Waldorf educational philosophy (Uhrmacher, 1995). This Waldorf pedagogy strives to develop students' intellectual, artistic, and practical skills in an integrated and holistic manner. The cultivation of students' imagination and creativity is a central focus. In the Waldorf philosophy, individual teachers and schools have a great deal of autonomy in determining curriculum content, teaching methodology, and governance. Qualitative assessments of student work are integrated into the daily life of the classroom. Quantitative testing plays a minimal role. The educational goal is to provide the students with a basis on which to develop into free, morally responsible, and integrated individuals, thus also helping them to go out into the world as free, independent and creative beings.

The anthroposophical philosophy to science and science education is often interwoven with a phenomenological approach. The main aim is to cultivate a sense of wholeness with regard to the human's place in nature. UW/H was not a part of a formal Waldorf system, but it is founded and rooted in this tradition. The integration of head, heart, and hands is important in the anthroposophical tradition. These formulations also became important for me, and they influenced my way of approaching students and research. When meeting students as well as other people, I want to start by meeting their hearts.

Humboldtian Ideals and Witten Values[3]

My favorite way of teaching is "fireplace discussions." One variant of this is the "walking around" or being together method. This means teaching through direct interaction and dialogue with the students.

> I enjoyed your "walking around method" either in Rome, Ruhr or other places—in one of the Rome seminars you gave instructions to focus on three questions with one walking partner that we did not know beforehand; [it] was quite inspiring. (Hannah Möltner, 2019)[4]

---

[2] The presentation in these paragraphs is leaning on www.uni-wh.de/ universitaet/ accessed August 22, 2019. See also Wikipedia.

[3] See previous footnote.

[4] See discussion of Dr Hannah Möltner later in this chapter.

I am trying to apply this at all levels. The fireplace discussion method of teaching is rooted in a Humboldtian research tradition. UW/H has been considered as an idealistic model for the future of German higher education, but it has also been considered as a challenge to the German higher education system. The university is recognized as one of Germany's few private universities considered as "Humboldtian" and as a role model in terms of course structure, integration of practical and theoretical training, and innovative approaches to payment of tuition fees.

Common features in Humboldtian seminar-type teaching are lecturing in small, collaborative groups and a high level of commitment among the students. The students should be independent and responsible, and the teaching should be based on self-directed learning. The students should study the original sources in the discipline, and there should be a strong connection between the seminar work and the research practices of the discipline (Kruse, 2006: 348).

UW/H presents three main values that adhere to this educational concept from anthroposophy and the Humboldtian tradition: encouraging freedom, striving for truth, and assuming social responsibility.

- Freedom from state regulation is seen as an opportunity for responsible organization of curricula, research, and university management. UW/H provides a suitable context for all its members to develop special competences and pursue personal ideals for the benefit of society and environment, under conditions of autonomy and equality. UW/H promotes an understanding of other cultures and encourages other universities to expand and redefine freedom for students and researchers alike, with visible consequences for the society as a whole.
- The quest for truth goes beyond feasibility. UW/H stands for a pluralistic approach and encourages personal experience, methodical changes in perspective, and open dialogue between disciplines as preconditions for sound judgement. It thus integrates problem-oriented approaches, assessments, and findings, whose possible consequences for society and environment are carefully evaluated. UW/H sees itself as an institution of lifelong learning.
- Freedom is contingent upon responsibility. Members of UW/H assume personal responsibility for what they do and for sustained development of their university as a role model for university reform in Germany. The privilege of education in freedom implies social responsibility and an obligation to demonstrate exceptional commit-

ment to the common good in society, environment, and the scientific community.

I found UW/H to have the features of a lighthouse in showing the direction for true scholarship. This scholarship goes beyond learning the tricks of the trade in order to publish. It is holistic, and we cannot split our scholarly lives and ourselves as private persons. True scholarship is our lives.

Elite University and Business Leaders

There are three faculties at UW/H: the faculty of health, the faculty of humanities and arts, and the faculty of management and economics. Students must take courses from more than one faculty. "Thursday is Stufu-day (Studium Fundamentale) for all students of Witten/Herdecke University. Students of all faculties meet for general studies in liberal arts and humanities and work together on topics concerning society and culture, philosophy and history, literature and arts, as well as economy and health."[5] Here, they can choose a topic of interest from a broad range of courses and usefully complement their studies this way. Within the context of these general studies, the students discuss current issues and challenges and enhance their own communication skills. Art courses such as theater acting, singing, dancing, or sculpting complement the educational concept of the Studium Fundamentale. This holistic approach has been considered groundbreaking.

I worked in the faculty of management and economics, and most of the time I held the Reinhard Mohn Endowment Chair of Management, Business Ethics and Societal Change. It was thus on my table also to contribute to societal change—to contribute to making a better world.

One of the particular features of the university was the Family Business Institute. Many of the leading family businesses in Germany had funded this institute for family businesses, and many leading business families in Germany sent their children to UW/H—not to become financiers or consultants, but to become responsible citizens and business leaders. My role, and that of the university, was to train the students to become the business leaders of the future. The values of freedom, truth and social

---

[5]   www.uni-wh.de/en/uwh-international/university/faculty-of-humanities -and-arts/ accessed August 15, 2019.

responsibility were given top priority in the communication to and with the students.

I enjoyed teaching the bachelor and master students, but I tried to follow a teaching philosophy based on dialogue and interaction. I wanted to follow the anthroposophical and Humboldtian research traditions. This required work in small groups, and with students who were prepared. This is still my lecturing and learning philosophy.

THE WITTEN SEMINARS

Running seminars for younger colleagues became my main role at UW/H. They were labeled the Witten seminars. Alvesson and Gabriel (2013) suggest:

> Institutions and associations should perhaps run courses and workshops on idea generations and communication. At present, publication forms seem to matter more than ends (having something to say). Senior scholars should encourage PhD students and junior scholars to discover their voice in meaningful and important things they want to say, rather than obsession about adapting to conventional journal publication norms. (Alvesson and Gabriel, 2013: 257)

This also describes how the Witten seminars developed.

The Witten seminars were usually weekend seminars. Most of them took place at UW/H, but we had also some seminars at collaborating Italian universities. There were usually four to six seminars per year. We had "research publication and the international academic community" (RPIAC) seminars, "value-creating board" (VCB) seminars, and "women on boards" (WoB) seminars. The audience changed over the years, and varied depending on topic. Some of the seminars were compulsory for my PhD students, but we also invited other scholars from around the world to participate. Most came from European countries. I used to invite scholars with whom I had a mentoring relationship. Some of the events were adapted so that they could be more attractive to practitioners. The number of participants varied from fewer than 10 to around 30. Usually I had a colleague from outside Germany to coteach with me and my assistant professors.

Dr. Hannah Möltner, now a professor at FOM in Essen, was one of my colleagues at UW/H. She wrote the following reflections about the Witten seminars:

> During Morten's time in Witten, a sharing philosophy was formulated and put into practice. I had the pleasure to join some of the Witten seminars—we discussed our research, strived for meaningful research and exchanged reflections on current trends in international academia. The Witten seminars provided time and space for a sharing approach in research and attracted PhDs, post-docs, and senior scholars. Some of the ties formed back then last until today and keep on being a great source of inspiration! (Hannah Möltner, 2019)

Passion and Compassion—Head, Heart, and Hands

All the Witten seminars started with a welcome reception in my offices, most often with sparkling wine. During this reception, the participants introduced themselves. I usually presented some of the grand challenges being faced in the region, and how this should influence our lives and research. Most often I also used my glass of sparkling wine to say, with Johan Wolfgang Goethe, that "life is too short to drink bad wine," leading to some reflections about the urgency of doing important things, as well as working with people who give us energy. I focused on the need to have a heart for people and compassion for each other.

I wanted to fuel in the junior scholars the natural desire to make a difference. I wanted them to become, in the terms of Alvesson and Gabriel, committed social scholars rather than article producing technicians. Instead of socializing students into the chase for prestigious journal publications, we tried to support them to achieve their desire to make a difference. I wanted the PhD students to combine PhD training with developing their own research agendas, around their own hearts.

The integration of head, heart, and hands was important in the Witten seminars. During my period in Witten and around the Witten seminars, I started to define myself as a mentor. Being a mentor is different from being a sponsor or a coach. A mentor has a long-term perspective on developing the persons being supported. In my own research, teaching, and mentoring I have now a policy of starting with the heart. Being a mentor is about working with the heart.

Open Innovation

During one of the Witten seminars, some of the participants started to define what we were doing as open innovation. We invited everybody to share his or her work. Some were mature scholars and were far into their careers or actual projects; others were younger in their academic careers or in their projects. Nobody was afraid that someone might steal his or her ideas or projects. We all placed them on the table so that everybody could help in developing them, learn from them, or possibly use them in their own thinking and writing. There are risks and advantages in using open processes rather than closing doors. However, reciprocal trust and communities of scholars had been created through this sharing philosophy. Personally, I hardly published with any of the participants, but they found each other and continued working together. Academic communities were developed.

A SHARING COMMUNITY

The final part of the scholarly ecosystem presented in this book is the community. It is defined by a sharing, impact-driven, and open philosophy. I will here come back to some of the sharing community reflections made by the outgoing AOM presidents, some of whom argued for a sharing and vibrant community with mutual respect, reciprocity, and enduring relationships, and that we as scholars should share with one another what truly matters, have community conversations, and demonstrate a willingness as individual members to share with one another.

One of the challenges I observed through my period in Germany was how some senior professors used their PhD students as "slaves" to support their own research and publication record. This was against my understanding of true scholarship. Senior faculty and professors should use their time, experience, and power to empower PhD students and junior faculty. Senior faculty should strive to improve the research environment for junior faculty so they can realize their intellectual ideals and become the best they can be (Chen, 2014; Tsui, 2013; Whetten, 2001). The community should be impact-driven, with a compassion for a sustainable future, and educate minds while educating hearts, always aspiring to be better human beings. Doctoral students should be challenged to find their calling and follow their hearts (Tsui, 2013; Whetten, 2001: 178). Any academic field that exists to satisfy itself and only its own interests will soon have few resources (Hambrick, 1994: 16). Tung

(2005: 243) cited Desmond Tutu: "A person is a person through other persons." The community should be openminded, supporting team-based research to conduct programmatic scholarship, and should educate members about the value of adopting different research models (DeNisi, 2010; Lee, 2009; Smith, 2008). We should develop a community that enables collective action and change (Glynn, 2019). The time horizon for this is our entire academic life (Bartunek, 2003). We need personal engagement and job engagement displayed by the use of head, heart, and hands (Shapiro, 2017). We need a society that goes beyond "winner takes all." Research will benefit from interaction and learning from each other, and collegiums should be built from the bottom up.

Tsui argued for the need to replace the "value free ideal" with thoughtfully developed values (Tsui, 2018: 419), and through responsible science, business schools can truly become positive forces of change and contribute to the creation of a sustainable future for humanity as a whole (Tsui, 2018: 419).

In this chapter I have shown how my experiences from UW/H and Germany have shaped my methods of formulating, exploring, and developing our academic community. Concepts such as developing the heart, grand challenges, social engagement, and holistic, reflexive, and open innovation approaches have been illustrated as ways to resolve the crisis in research. I have emphasized the open innovation approach in a sharing philosophy. The open approach includes a dialogue where all participants are open to sharing and learning from each other, and even to being changed through the conversation.

Many of the Witten seminar participants have continued to see each other regularly at the EURAM meetings.

8.   An impact-driven approach—making a change

MAKING A BETTER WORLD—SOCIALLY COMMITTED SCHOLARSHIP

MacIntosh et al. (2017) edited a special issue of the *British Journal of Management* with the following title: "Impact and Management Research: Exploring Relationships between Temporality, Dialogue, Reflexivity and Praxis." This title would also have been appropriate for this chapter. This chapter is about an impact-driven approach to doing management research. How, when, and for whom does our research make an impact? Our research should be fueled by natural desire to make an impact or make a difference. Impact appears over time, and we should consider our impact through lifelong scholarship.

Our scholarship is changing and developing over time, and we should aim at a longitudinal immersion of engaged scholarship (Wells and Nieuwenhuis, 2017). It will usually be noticed whether you do your research for your own benefit, or instead to achieve a higher objective. Throughout this chapter, I follow the examples and experiences of my work about women on boards (WoB). At the end of the chapter, I present some examples of polymorphic research and how it stimulates the relaxation of some assumptions in the debate and research about WoB.

At the beginning of the 1990s I was working at Nordland Research Institute and Bodø Graduate School of Business (now a part of Nord University, Norway), where I taught a master course on boards of directors. Åshild Nordnes was one of my students, and she wrote her master thesis on women on boards. Åshild was also a colleague of mine at Nordland Research Institute. However, her concern was not only for her own studies. She was already an experienced board member, and she had a feminist agenda in getting more women on boards. She included me in her agenda. She was the activist, I became her mentor, and together we started something that could be labeled action research. We acted based on scholarly knowledge, and we tried to learn from the processes and the outcomes. I learned much from her and our joint activities. This was the beginning of my research agenda about women on boards. Through this agenda, I wanted to do something important for society.

LONGITUDINAL WORK WITH PRACTITIONERS

Action Research—Research with Practitioners

Rigor requires a research design that depends on relevance (Starkey, Hatchuel, and Tempest, 2009: 555). Rigor in management research may be conceptualized as combinations of different types of interactions between the researchers and their objects. Action research is collaboration between researchers and practitioners with the purpose of creating scientifically rigorous research and relevant practice. Action research is multidisciplinary, and the actual project often concentrates on context rather than generalizations.

Research *with* practitioners is even more problematic than applied research *for* practitioners. Such collaborative research implies that the results should fit into the system of science as well as meeting the needs of the practitioners. Thus, collaborative research has to be understood as applied research informed through cooperation with practitioners. Confusion may easily arise when researchers become involved in practice with practitioners. In some of my earlier projects, I reported on the problems of combining the identities of a dedicated researcher and a dedicated practitioner (Huse, 1996).

As noted, my research agenda about women on boards (WoB) started alongside Åshild Nordnes in 1990. I had already discussed a potential country comparative project about WoB with Idie Kesner,[1] and I undertook various demographic mapping studies and business case studies about WoB. I started teaching a master course about the Scandinavian leadership model and female leadership. Through my research, I argued that board performance would improve with more women on boards and in leadership positions. Thus, efforts should be made to increase the number of women on boards (Bilimoria and Huse, 1997; Gabrielsson and Huse, 2002; Huse, 1993). In the mid 1990s I also started applying for research funding for this topic, made conference presentations, got

---

[1]   At that time at the University of North Carolina at Chapel Hill.

involved in training programs for women to reach "the top," and started advising politicians and creators of public policy in Norway on how to get more women on boards. This activity was documented in the daily newspapers and popular press.[2] In the mid 1990s I also became the president of StyreAkademiet (the National Association of Directors) in Norway, and increasing the number of women on boards became a part of StyreAkademiet's agenda. We wanted to see more WoB in Norway in general, but in our own organization in particular. At the Academy of Management (AOM) meeting in 1998, I was a part of a symposium about women on boards. This symposium included several important scholars—for example, Sue Vinnicombe and Diana Bilimoria, as well as Mary Mattis from Catalyst.

From 1996 to 2001, I had a part-time professorship in Sweden. Sweden was more advanced than Norway in terms of doing something for women's entrepreneurship and women in business leadership, including women on boards. Several of my projects about getting women on boards took place in Sweden in this period—through interviews, tutoring master students, evaluating mentorship projects, and teaching on training seminars for WoB. I also found the public discussion in Sweden very interesting. There was debate as to whether Sweden should introduce a gender quota law to support getting women on boards. My agenda to increase discussion around gender quotas developed considerably then. I started advising the Norwegian government about a board gender quota regulation as a possible instrument in Norway. In 2000, at the AOM conference in Toronto, I gave a symposium presentation focusing on the role of quotas and other public policy instruments for getting more women on boards.

Mentoring Champions: Second and Third-Order Impact

At the beginning of this chapter, I presented Åshild. I did not really understand until later that I had an informal mentoring relationship with her. Later I had other, similar relationships. I was approached by, and got to know, women who wanted to combine academic degrees with business or political agendas about boards of directors. Tone Veen was one of them. In the mid 1990s she had just started a consultancy with the aim of recruiting women to boards. For me it was an important experience to

---

[2]   For example, in Juss-kontakt, Aftenposten, and so on.

follow her, learning about her thinking, reflecting with her, and joining her in organizing events to attract attention to her business.

From 2001 until 2012, I worked as a part-time professor at various universities in Italy. Research and various discussions on WoB increased in importance in this period. Casual meetings and discussions with some people led me to other people, and without reflecting on it, I became involved in the political WoB debate in Italy. Mentoring relations developed with two women at the interface of academia/business/politics. Independently, both of them led me to Fondazione Marisa Bellisario and its founder and president, Lella Golfo. Fondazione Bellisario is "the oldest and most influential association of Italian women, an authentic 'lobby of merit' and a real hotbed of female leadership."[3] The foundation supports the professionalism of women and promotes a culture of gender equality, focusing on the need for deep equality in society. The mission of the foundation is to draw the attention of the political and business worlds, institutions, and enterprises to promote the role of professional women.

Following these Italian women individually was a tremendous holistic learning experience for me. I was able to learn about how they thought, their motivations, their actions and interactions with others. I was included as a discussant partner, an academic alibi, and support for organizing events and in that way attracting attention to their initiatives. I started to see that in practice, I was again involved in action research. As some women in Germany approached me, I developed this action research approach more systematically to make a country comparative action research project: "Exploring actors, their motivations and interactions in efforts to get quotas for women on boards." My role was to mentor advocates or champions for change.

The design of this project involved collaboration with colleagues at universities in different countries; they would support me with an infrastructure, including input to the national context and national networks. I also expected that they would be important for identifying possible advocates for change with whom I could work. Initiatives started in several countries, but I undertook full projects in Germany, Spain, and Slovenia. They supplemented my earlier experiences from Scandinavia and Italy.

---

[3]   www.fondazionebellisario.org/online/en/presidente/ accessed during April 2019.

An ERC Advanced Grant to follow up these ideas was applied for in 2015. The application was declined. I applied for another ERC Advanced Grant in 2018, redirecting the grant application toward a focus on second and third-order effects and contributing to changing the game of research. The second application was also declined. However, in 2018 I was invited to lead a consortium for an EQUIP grant application among universities in European countries and India. We submitted the proposal "Creating a mission for reaching a vision of sustainable wellbeing: Rethinking boards, equality and CSR." The project was a collaboration among leading scholars from universities in Finland, India, Norway, Slovenia, and the United Kingdom. This application was not successful either, but all three project application processes had significant learning value.

TEMPORALITY IN RESEARCH—WOMEN ON BOARDS

Dialogic Trading Zones

Dialogic trading zones are places where academics and practitioners can work together over time (Romme et al., 2015). Through my research, I wanted to have an impact on practice. Practical impact is not something that only should be considered or added after a research project or publication has been conducted—something that follows after a study has been completed. It should be included in the project design and in the research process. This is what Cunliffe and Scaratti (2017) address as temporality in research, and they argue for research in which, over time, practitioners and academics are engaged in the situation in which the knowledge is produced.

Sue Vinnicombe and others, in Sealy et al. (2017), use the concept of dialogic trading zones for impactful research, taking their experience with research about WoB as their case. They emphasize the importance of time spent in the relationship with practitioners, and trace their work over 15 years. The dialogic trading zones argument is that exchange and coproduction of knowledge between scholars and practitioners should be based on long-term crossfertilizations. Sealy et al. argue that the understanding of who should be in the trading zone should not be restrictive, and will expand over time.

WoB Cruise Workshops

In 2008, I was contacted by Innovation Norway, an industry development agency in Norway, to undertake research about WoB. When designing and developing this project, I invited various colleagues and students, some from other countries, for a workshop. For budget reasons, but also as a play on words, I decided to organize this workshop on a cruise ship. This was our first Women on Board cruise research workshop. I organized this workshop for ten years in total, in most cases on cruises between Oslo/Norway and Copenhagen/Denmark or Kiel/Germany. The participants were all invited as contributors to a joint project about women on boards. The workshops largely did not consider writing or publishing, but rather developing research projects to make an impact on the discussions about WoB. We tried to keep the number of participants at around ten, and some became regulars, even though most years we focused on new projects.

The early workshops, as well as one later one, had a focus on exploring "The golden skirts." The main method was interviews with women who were members of several boards. Other workshops were dedicated to exploring methods to increase the number of WoB. Some of these projects were crossnational, and all projects integrated micro-level perspectives to understand boards and getting women on boards. Some years we focused on research about the consequences and introductions of quotas for getting WoB. The cruise workshop one year was dedicated to the EQPOWEREC project.[4] This was a knowledge transfer from Norway to Slovenia about WoB and gender equality. Outcomes from several of the workshops are summarized in Huse (2018b).

The cruise workshops were for researchers, but several times we combined the research workshops with research/practice/politics events or think tanks, organized in Norway or Germany. One of these events is documented in Machold et al. (2013): "Getting women on to corporate boards: A snowball starting in Norway." Adjunct with the workshops we sometimes also organized PhD courses about WoB. This meant that in practice, over the years a large number of researchers, PhD students,

---

[4]   For EQPOWEREC see for example www.norwaygrants.si/2009-2014/ en/projects/programme-nor-fm-projects/eqpowerec/ or www.facebook.com/ Eqpowerec/ accessed August 15, 2019.

and WoB activists became part of our WoB network. One of them was Johanna Degen, a German psychologist at the University of Flensburg:

> Attending the WOB seminar as a psychologist among management scholars I experienced and integrated the real life experience of the overcome of scientific disciplines and the creation of possibilities. Disciplines as spheres on their own are nowadays outdated, not in the way that we are not experts with specific knowledge and focus, but in the way that we depend on each other to create holistic content and meaning in a rhizomatic research culture.[5] Following that we were all melted together as equal individuals with equal perspectives, developing solutions and new knowledge and skills—nourishing each other, not fighting each other's truths. We are all together on one mission: making an impact, seeking to understand world, recreating the notion of world from different angles, learning from each other. This way of thinking science became clear and palpable as a practical example. Management scholar, psychology scholar, there was no difference, no opposition. In addition, what I argue and experience is not an interdisciplinary attempt, it is the disruption of disciplines. That maybe because we are commonly human sciences. This is plain: How to understand management, how to research boards without taking the subjective perspective into serious account? How to take subjective sovereignty in tension to social norms into account without seeing it from the sociologist's perspective? However, it is more complex than that and regards all disciplines: even the physicist has to consider his own impact—understanding that some molecules only move when a human eye looks at them. Reflecting on that the truth lies in him as subject in tension with the world and the notion of it. Even the psychologist cannot understand subjects without understanding logical interactions between objects and scientific laws, which are forming and sometimes determining the environment of the subject's becoming.
>
> Reflecting on the self and the impact of subjective sovereignty and norms and tensions can be life, scholar, and method-changing. WoB was the place and space where the theoretical idea of overcoming discipline and even interdisciplinarity was manifested as real life experience. (Johanna Degen, 2019)

Redirecting a Research Agenda

My research about women on boards has been changing over recent years. The WoB cruise workshops have contributed to that. I have been building on earlier experiences and research, but research topics, theories, methods, and interpretations are significantly different today from what they were 10–15 years ago. I have been moving away from meso-level studies with a focus on the relationships between women on boards

---

[5]   See Guerin (2013).

and board or company performance. Now I place greater emphasis on integrating micro- and macro-level perspectives. Some examples follow.

Alongside colleagues, I have undertaken several studies that aim to go beyond a superficial analysis and attempt to better understand the political, social, and cultural dynamics that underpin the increase in the number of WoB. One of the most significant publications from this study is Seierstad et al. (2017), which draws on an analysis of political games to understand the dynamics underpinning the introduction of a national quota. In this publication, we explored the role of different actors and processes by studying the developments in Norway, England, Germany, and Italy. The study employed a processual research design, and mapped the political games behind, inside, and outside legislative areas.

In other studies, we explored characteristics of WoB. What do we know about the women who are board members and those becoming board members? What are their backgrounds? What are their challenges, characteristics, and contributions? Does it matter if the women are recruited in a tokenistic fashion or because of a quota law? I have in the international press been called the "golden skirts" professor. That relates to a study about the human capital characteristics of women getting multiple board memberships because of the board gender quota regulation in Norway (Huse, 2011; 2012b). In a study of Italian "golden skirts," we combined institutional theory and social capital theory. We found that the social capital of the women in this group changed depending on institutional pressure (Rigolini and Huse, 2019).

Has this redirected agenda resulted in a new stream of research? Should the outcome of this redirection be seen as a new research stream? There is a coherence to these studies, and they represent something hardly addressed in mainstream research about WoB.

A first key attribute of studies in this agenda is their objective to make a change in order to contribute to a sustainable society. Their designs are impact-driven.

Second, they are developed with close attention to practice, and even in collaboration with practitioners. They are developed within a dialogic trading zone, and often in longitudinal work with practitioners.

Third, they are dynamic and build on temporality in research. The single projects do not stand alone, but build on and in communication with similar studies. The impact will be shown over time and developed together with similar studies, more than based on one single publication.

Fourth, they are leaning on a sharing philosophy of doing research, including that of being communal and open in addition to that of being impact-driven. The studies are not for individual credit, but represent a joint effort in making a change.

Fifth, they are venturesome and follow the recommendation to do polymorphic research.

POLYMORPHIC RESEARCH

Alternative Ways of Thinking and Doing Research

Alvesson, Gabriel, and Paulsen (2017) suggested the use of polymorphism to achieve meaningful and innovative research. The major point of polymorphism is to open up alternative ways of thinking and writing research. It is vital for the academic community to develop good scholarship, including developing innovative ideas, practicing reflexivity, and writing creatively (Alvesson and Sandberg, 2013).

In polymorphic research, we break with the mainstream and explore new ways of applying theories and methods, target audiences, and ways of dissemination. We move from procedures and techniques to reflexivity. We are not gap spotting, but rather challenging assumptions.

In my research about value-creating boards, I collected new and alternative ways of doing research. My research on WoB is even more radical. I have applied the "champagne method," and have used my knowledge and skills in mentoring women advocating for change through action research. In order to understand the implications of polymorphic research, I will here present examples of how we can challenge assumptions, methods, interpretations, and communication.

Challenging Assumptions

Are the assumptions in the Women on Board debate and research sustainable? I am committed to contributing to a sustainable society, wellbeing, and gender equality. In research about WoB there is an assumption that women are discriminated against. Is this correct? Are all arguments for getting women on boards correct and sustainable? Will I be harming that and those I want to support if I question these assumptions? In addition, how to avoid harm and still make an important topic tangible? How can a male scholar fully understand and argue female perspectives? From a sustainability perspective, I am still questioning many of the arguments and assumptions in the political, public, and academic debates about

WoB. I am also entering the space of normative unsayable topics. Three examples follow.

My first example is inspired by the book of a Danish scholar (Rennison, 2012). I used her five main codes to sort the discussion in various countries about WoB: biological, talent, utility, exclusion, and freedom codes. Rennison applies sociological system theory. She argues that each code may have validity in itself, but some of the combinations of them are not sustainable. She suggests that combinations of the various codes of arguments may, for example, lead to comfortable blindness, complementary mutualism, contradictory controversies, cynical parasitism, or creative misunderstanding.

The biological code is based on popularly reported views on the different roles that men and women play in society. Broad, and often historical, stereotypes hold that women are traditionally "homemakers" and men the breadwinners. This code is strongly associated with religious conservative environments. It has been viewed as antifeminist and excessively conservative. The talent code has a meritocratic perspective but may also be regarded as somewhat paternalistic. It is often focused on "training" women to learn the skillsets of men in business. Women identifying with this code do not want to be seen as "quota women," where representation is based on tokenism. The utility code is based on an underlying assumption that women and men are different and can make distinctive contributions as leaders. Under this code, leadership has stereotypically been viewed as a male domain linked to resources and positionality, while the distinct leadership skills of women are seen as an underutilized resource for businesses. The exclusion code is about collective feminism: "Women are being discriminated against, the glass ceiling and various institutional barriers are apparent. The system needs to be fixed." In contrast, the freedom code is based on women already having the freedom to choose—even how to experience gender. The code is considered by many as antifeminist and individualistic.

Applying the system theory in my action research projects in various countries led me to the following analyses. Much of the international debate surrounding how women's representation on boards and business leadership can be increased is characterized by creative misunderstandings. This is reflected in the presentations by Sheryl Sandberg (2013). In Norway, the combination of codes could be characterized as comfortable blindness. This is where codes coexist alongside each other with little imperative for change. Contradictory controversies occur when the representatives of the different codes are in implacable conflicts (often displayed in Germany), and cynical parasitism is when the one code infects the logic of another (for example in Spain). The Complementary mutualism takes place when both stand to benefit from the presence of the other, while constructive alliances are when a pattern is observed, and connections are made across the various codes. The latter two, as we indicated in the case of Italy and Slovenia, may have the highest productivity potential and be the most sustainable for progressing women onto boards. A main feature in Italy was how different stances were openly addressed and understood, and complemented each other without detailed coordination efforts. The case in Slovenia highlighted how different stances were accepted and alliances were developed in order to achieve progress.

The second example comes from one of my German female executive PhD students, writing about the talent pipeline for becoming a board member. She has positioned her work within the label of the "academic housewife." She argues that I am the academic housewife, while she is in the corporate career pipeline. In our work together, we analyze holes in the corporate pipelines, from those met by teenagers to those met by workers considering retirement. We conclude that gender equality in top corporate positions will not occur before women and men face a similar amount of holes in their career pipelines. Today, in most countries, women have many more holes in the career pipeline. Some holes are more attractive than others, and some are considered negative. Through our pipeline analysis we want to explore whether, in many countries, in reality men rather than women are discriminated against. A main criterion for getting a board or top corporate position is gender, and it is now almost impossible for men to get such positions. If there is some truth to these assumptions, then changes in research focus are needed.

The third example comes from two Italian female scholars that wanted to do research with me about WoB and relational capital. Relational capital is different from human capital and social capital. Relational capital is about the way people interact with each other. The scholars argued that Italian women might have more relational capital than women in many other countries, which may have consequences for their actual board behavior and board contributions. We presented a paper proposal on this idea at some research workshops, and twice were asked if we knew about the work of Catherine Hakim from the London School of Economics. She has written about erotic capital (Hakim, 2011) and the title of one of her books is *Erotic Capital: The Power of Attraction in the Boardroom and the Bedroom*. She asks why some people seem to live charmed lives, and responds that erotic capital is an overlooked human asset.

In a previous study about gender dynamics (Huse and Solberg, 2006) I reported that we must seek to understand the impact flirtation may have on board performance. However, while some will identify with women's ability to use their erotic capital as an asset, I want to draw attention to erotic capital as an asset also for men—for making careers and even for getting to board positions. We must then try to understand how erotic capital is similar to or different from relational and social capital, and if erotic capital may in practice replace or support the human capital of the board members. One of the challenges for myself and my colleagues is whether we want to be labeled as "erotic capital scholars." However, erotic capital should not be understood as sleeping one's way to the boardroom.

Challenging Methods—Vodka and Champagne

A few years ago I started to challenge the environment by talking about my "champagne method" in my studies of WoB, and began using it in an explicit and conscious way. I had discovered that much of the knowledge I acquired had come through conversations with women with board experience, women aspiring for board positions, or women advocating for doing something for other women. Many of these conversations were not recorded, and often I did not take any immediate physical notes. However, these conversations helped me to understand many issues around their ambitions, their challenges, their interactions, and themselves. In most cases, I had to pay for the champagne. It was expensive, but paid off in terms of research insights.

I think I started to use this term after somebody presented the "Finnish interview method" concept. Finns are known for not speaking much in formal settings, also in formal interviews. However, as soon as the tape recorder is turned off, and beer and vodka have been placed on the table and consumed, the interviewees typically start to reveal deeper layers of information about interesting and important issues.

During my board of directors research, I have experienced different types of ethnographic method. I have been involved in "fly on the wall" studies, "one of the lads" studies and "following directors" studies, and have experience with videotaping, tape recording, using notebooks, and taking notes. Through the champagne method, I learned the importance of continuous reflection, and of relating the inputs from the various conversations to my existing knowledge and experiences.

The champagne method eased my concerns about connecting to my own experiences. It made inner transfers possible by melting boundaries. The champagne method became an important approach in my action research project about mentoring advocates for change. It made me connect on a deeper level, and it contributed to building trust and relation between a scholar as a person and a participant as a person—entering human levels on trust.

After a faculty seminar where I presented the champagne method for doing research about WoB, I was invited to join a project on introspection. One person in the audience found that my champagne method approach had much to do with introspection.

Challenging Interpretations—Introspection

In polymorphic research, we are being reflexive and self-critical. We are bringing in uncertainty and our thoughts. I approach this through introspection. I have been using introspection as a method when writing this book, and even in this chapter about impact and WoB. Introspection is a process whereby I am observing my own conscious thoughts and emotions. Introspection helps me interpret and understand my observations or data. In introspection, I am critically engaging with self-knowledge, and thus vulnerable to changing even myself. This happens when understanding my position in the field and the impact of the self and its becoming connect with the constructed truth. It happens when something becomes explicit, intersubjective, transparent and, due to that, understandable, instead of being a hidden bias.

Introspection can be understood as mindfulness, meditation, reflectiveness, or retrospection. There are similarities between these concepts. Introspection has a focus on content. The content matters. Introspection involves active thought processes and investigation of our thoughts, emotions, and memories. Mindfulness, when compared to introspection, pays less attention to content, which may be irrelevant. Being able to watch the thoughts and emotions arise and pass away is more important than understanding the content. Making introspection explicit helps both to connect inner processes and content and the reciprocal impact of that, and the notion of world becoming.

Introspection and meditation are very different from each other. In introspection, we are remembering something we did or something that happened in the past. We consider it from different perspectives: what went wrong, was it my fault or someone else's, can it be improved in the future, and so on. In meditation, we are not thinking about anything in particular. We are not resisting any thoughts that come to our mind. These may be unconscious thoughts. In introspection we act, for example, to try to find the whys, and the pluses and minuses.

Reflection can mean introspection, but it can also mean recalling the past, or simply thinking about something. Introspection is about self-analysis, where we are trying to recall and analyze our own thoughts or emotions. It is an inner insight for us and others, making the subject (more) transparent—our position in the world, environment, and relationships, including all inner reactions.

Retrospection is about reconstructing what has previously happened, while introspection is about analyzing or examining our emotions, actions, and thoughts, and thinking deeply about what has caused them. Through introspection, I have become more aware of how I deal with data and observations. I do not take my data as objective facts, but I am conscious that I interpret them based on my previous knowledge and experience. I multiply their worth through the subjective perspective.

Challenging Communication

Since 2000, I have given about 150 presentations and speeches about WoB or getting more WoB (Huse, 2015) in more than 20 countries. These come in addition to international scientific conference presentations. Among these presentations we find speeches in the British, Italian, and Slovenian parliaments; at various political events or for politicians and governmental bodies in Germany, the Netherlands, Spain, and Scotland; in various financial institutions such as the Luxembourg Stock Exchange, Qatar Financial Market Authorities, Bank of England, Bank of Thailand, and Consob in Italy; and in many meetings with women's or gender equality organizations, business and industry associations, and universities, including many international women's day arrangements. Can such research dissemination be compared to "A-journal hits"? For me these events are learning processes in themselves. I have most likely learned a lot from listening to about 500 presentations made about women on boards; I have learned from preparing and developing my presentations; and not least, I have learned a lot from the interactions with the audiences in the different places. Thus, I started to sort my experiences, and tested and refined my arguments and observations through my speeches and in the dialogues with the various audiences. These observations were combined with more than a hundred interviews in several countries. These and similar observations have been presented to critical scholarly, practitioner, and activist audiences during my several speeches and discussions.

It is not straightforward to apply WoB lessons from one country directly to another. Indeed, a number of quite fundamental questions need to be addressed. They include what a board is, what a quota is, and, strangely enough, what a woman is. It is also important to understand variations in national and institutional contexts, including corporate structures.

WHAT REALLY MATTERS—MAKING A CHANGE

How, when, and for whom does our research make an impact? Socially committed scholarship is important for me. However, we should also think in second and third-order effects. The outgoing AOM presidents formulated that our research must have value for further research (Lee, 2009; Smith, 2008), and our work should make the world a better place (Cummings, 2007; McGahan, 2018). Impact occurs over time and involves engagement of both practitioners and academics in the situation in which the knowledge is being produced (Cunliffe and Scaratti, 2017). Impacts happen over time, and scholarship is generated over a career, not through a few "A-hits."

What has become apparent in the debates about increasing the representation of WoB is that the business case is just one imperative. While this has been a core aspect of the argument for increased representation, larger goals are also important, including societal sustainability, equity and equality, and wellbeing. Getting more WoB and quotas for increasing the number of WoB must be evaluated based on its contribution to society and future generations.

9.   A new ecosystem equilibrium—true scholarship

RITORNO AL PASSATO

Ritorno al passato is the name of a restaurant in Rome. For several years, I used to use this restaurant as an office space. *Ritorno al passato* is located in front of the Pantheon, which is considered by many, including myself, as the center of Rome. Going back in time, this was also the center of western civilization. In this book, I go back to some of the roots of our reflections about "true scholarship," and highlight how we have moved away from them. The core question in this book is how to return to true scholarship from the present publish or perish (POP) culture.

The legacy of Ernest L. Boyer has been a benchmark through much of this book. Boyer died in 1995. He had begun work on a book called *Scholarship Assessed*, but he died before it was finished. Some of his colleagues completed the book, but he was able to present his reflections about it in various public speeches before he died. Some of these speeches have been published (Boyer, 1996a; 1996b).

In his benchmark 1990 book *Scholarship Reconsidered*, Boyer presented what scholarship is, and he introduced the scholarships of discovery, integration, application, and teaching. In Boyer (1996b), he details and extends his reflections on what scholarship is, including making a distinction between the scholarships of discovery and integration on the one side and the scholarship of sharing of knowledge on the other. Publications and teaching are ways in which we as scholars communicate our research, but he argued that scholarship is "not a single part function, but a four part function with all parts inextricably interlocked" (1996a: 6). In one of his speeches about engaged scholarship he concluded that scholarship has to prove its own worth not on its own terms, but by service to the nation and the world (1996b: 33). The scholarship of application is the ultimate goal of our scholarly efforts.

For me, the main challenge in his latest work was that he reflected not only what scholarship is, but also what scholars are (Boyer, 1996a). This contains two main issues—the virtues appreciated, and the ways in which these virtues are assessed. He takes steps to get to the heart of a scholar's professional life.

Various virtues of scholars may be presented, such as honesty, courage, persistence, consideration, and humility (Boyer, 1996a: 9). Boyer would himself give priority to knowledgeability, integrity, and persistence. He summarized that assessments of scholars could be made through the following six evaluation criteria (1996a: 10):

- having a clearly stated scholarly goal;
- following well defined and appropriate procedures;
- having and using adequate resources;
- effectively communicating to others what scholarship is;
- achieving significant results;
- engaging in reflective self-critique.

He paused particularly at the last criterion and argued (1996a: 10):

> It seems very clear that we are able to advance scholarship only to the extent that those who engage in the act, whether it is research, teaching, or service, culminate their efforts in self-reflection: to look back, define strengths and weaknesses, and then to move forward to a higher level of performance, having learned from their own activities itself.

Assessments can be done through self-evaluation, peer evaluations, student evaluation and end-user evaluation. Boyer (1996a: 11–12) argues that publication is a self-evaluation, that peer evaluations should take place in mentoring relations within a culture of caring, and that context and time frame must be included in evaluations by present as well as former students.

I used an ecosystem thinking in the presentations in the first part of the book. I started this book by questioning whether true scholarship and academic research is in crisis, and I argued that true scholarship and our scholarly values are under attack. Today we have a scholarly ecosystem equilibrium that is upholding a publish or perish culture. Boyer's 1990 book was used by leaders of our scholarly associations, such as the Academy of Management, to define what true scholarship is, and they have held up warning signs about the present situation. They have expressed that efforts need to be made to return to true scholarship.

This is urgent, and we are now seeing several initiatives being taken to return to true scholarship. I showed in Chapter 5 how the various parts of the ecosystem are being approached. However, these efforts still require increased strength and coordination.

In Chapters 6, 7, and 8 of this book, I presented three cases for resolving the crisis by illustrating a "sharing philosophy" of doing research. These chapters not only illustrate many of the concepts and suggestions presented in the first part of the book, but also have a focus on the individual scholar in interaction with other scholars. They challenge us to reflect on what scholars are as well as what scholarship is. These chapters contribute to reflections about a new game of research—a game of research that is communal, open, and impact-driven—a sharing philosophy.

FROM THE POP CULTURE TO A SHARING PHILOSOPHY

The core message of the book is to move academia, and particularly the community of management scholars, from the POP culture back to true scholarship. My particular focus is on developing a sharing philosophy. In Table 9.1 I summarize the POP culture reality, the warnings from the AOM outgoing presidents, and various initiatives taken to return to meaningful research and true scholarship.

In the first column, I indicate the various parts of the scholarly ecosystem that this book is built around. In the second column, I present key words regarding the POP culture, as described in Chapter 2. The third column sets out frequent key comments from the addresses of the outgoing AOM presidents (Chapter 3). The last line of key comments for each ecosystem element is taken from Chapter 4 and the EURAM background. The third column summarizes the key actors and initiatives for resolving the crisis and changing the ecosystem. That column is a summary of Chapter 5, and it also includes the key elements of the sharing philosophy, which are communal, open, and impact-driven.

The second part of the book is about a community described by a sharing, impact-driven, and open philosophy. Some of the outgoing AOM presidents argued for a sharing and vibrant community with mutual respect, reciprocity, and enduring relationships. We as scholars should share with one another what truly matters, have community conversations, and show a willingness as individual members to share with one another. The community should be openminded, supporting team-based research to conduct programmatic scholarship and educate members

Table 9.1 *POP culture: summary*

	POP culture	Associations and presidents' reflections	Initiatives for change (examples)
Chapters	2 – Reality	3 and 4 (in italics) – Warnings and ambitions	5, 6, 7 and 8 – Initiatives
Institutions	Neoliberal market ideology	Accreditation systems and rankings are becoming threats to scholarly identity	National research evaluation systems (REF2021)
	New possibilities for evaluations		Open science:
	Pressure from accreditation agencies	Institutions are changing, but not in a positive way – challenging true scholarship	– FAIR
	Rankings and external incentives		– EU open access initiatives
	US based global standards	Collegiums should be built from the bottom up	
	A bureaucratic top-down approach	The present audit culture may be harmful to society	
	Tenure-track driven	*Collaboration across academic associations*	
Audience	Not meeting needs of practitioners	Theory and practice are not connected	Individual scholars
	A narrow group in academia	Get closer to practice	Journal and editors:
	A community of likely reviewers	Responsibility not to ourselves, but the world we live in	– Forums and special issues
	Those evaluating us	Research should not only contribute to a scientific discipline	Responsible Research in Business and Management (RRBM)
	Various pay-makers	Warning about the self-interested goal of promotion and tenure	AOM Practice Theme
	Not respected outside academia	*Dialogue between scholars, practitioners and policymakers*	
Message	Without relevance	Too narrow use of scholarship	Reshaping relevance and impact
	Incremental	We should see the whole and not only holes	Grand challenges:
	Gap spotting/seeking holes	Dare to care	– UN Sustainability Agenda
	Standardization	Doing research for the future	Returning to meaning and polymorphic research (Alvesson)
	Hiding work in progress	Inspire a better world	
	Short term and in the past	*Context-specific*	

	POP culture	Associations and presidents' reflections	Initiatives for change (examples)
Channel	Publication goal in itself	The way metrics is adapted is dysfunctional and US-centric	San Francisco Declaration (DORA)
	Focus on journals, but only	Research questions, methods and samples are often shaped by the	Beyond traditional metrics
	"A- journals"	choice of journals	(Harzing)
	Arbitrariness of journal rankings	Publications are only a minor part of doing research	
	English language journals	*Role in influencing standards*	
	Summarizing technical processes		
	Leading to scientific misconduct		
Community	Pressure facing scholarly values	Vibrant, supporting and sharing community of engaged scholars	AOM outgoing presidents: Passion
	Becoming publishing technicians	Senior faculty should support junior faculty	EURAM: Engaged scholars
	McDonaldism	We should educate minds by educating hearts,	A sharing philosophy
	Not appreciating scholarly maturity	Conduct team-based and programmatic	– A communal approach: Norefjell
	Loosing sense of community	We need a society that goes beyond "winner takes all."	– An open approach: Witten
	Relying on self—individualism	*Open, inclusive, cross-cultural and international*	– An impact-driven approach: WoB

about the value of adopting different research models (DeNisi, 2010; Lee, 2009; Smith, 2008). We should develop a community that enables collective action and change (Glynn, 2019).

The outgoing AOM presidents argued that doctoral students should be challenged to find their calling and follow their hearts (Tsui, 2013; Whetten, 2001: 178). Senior faculty should strive to achieve such a community. Senior faculty should improve the research environment for junior faculty so they can realize their intellectual ideals and become the best they can be (Chen, 2014; Tsui, 2013; Whetten, 2001). "We should see more scholastic coaching, more globally networked research teams, and more multidisciplinary and innovative co-creating" (Adler and Harzing, 2009: 91). We need personal engagement and job engagement displayed by the use of head, heart, and hands (Shapiro, 2017: 165). We need a society that goes beyond "winner takes all." Research will benefit from interaction and learning from each other. Ideas and possibilities will develop. Collegiums should be built from the bottom up. The time horizon for this is our entire academic life (Bartunek, 2003: 201–2).

Boyer (1990) suggested a sharing philosophy for doing management research. In their addresses, many of the previous AOM presidents not only presented their concerns about the future of our profession, but also suggested that a sharing philosophy could be a way of meeting the concerns (for example Chen, Cummings, Glynn, Ireland, Shapiro, Tsui, Tung, Van de Ven, and Whetten). In summary, this sharing philosophy can be characterized through:

- First, an open source/innovation approach, including open sources for research, learning, and innovation; leadership and liaising; venturesome research designs; holistic engagement and appreciation of diversity; and appreciating impacts in academia, business, and society.
- Second, a communal approach, including communal and joint credit, giving credit for research and not only for publications, and communities of engaged scholars.
- Third, an impact-driven approach, including evaluating research and impact on a long-term basis, appreciation of both in academia and practice, development of junior scholars, and multiplicative behavioral processes.

This is also in alignment with Alvesson and Sandberg (2013) and Alvesson, Gabriel, and Paulsen (2017).

The gap between the present status of the POP culture and the AOM presidents' reflections about the future of our profession emphasizes the urgent need for a new or alternative paradigm for developing management scholars, including PhD students and postdocs. Initiatives by DORA (the San Francisco Declaration) and RRBM (Responsible Research in Business and Management) are meeting questions about metrics and relevance (for example about message, audience, and channels). However, many of the previous presidents argued that additional steps might be required, including that of creating a new logic or philosophy for training and developing scholars (for example a sharing philosophy). There may be a need to change the game and to focus on what scholars *are*, rather than only describing functions of scholarship. This is also my main message in this book. This is the sharing philosophy.

"LIFE IS TOO SHORT TO DRINK BAD WINE"

Scholarship is not only what scholars *do*; it is what scholars *are*. In his presidential speech (Ireland, 2015), Duane Ireland noted that Boyer's types of scholarship could vary over time: "Some of us focus on only one or two types of scholarship at a point in time, whereas others of us may seek to balance our contributions across all four. Moreover, our focus on scholarship typically varies across the seasons of our careers" (Ireland, 2015: 153). I will now offer some reflections on how the evaluation of scholarship should vary and develop through our scholarly life cycle.

Adler, in his speech, emphasized the teaching mission of being a scholar, but also the importance of looking critically at our institutional context. He highlighted the damaging effect of the POP status hierarchy that elevates publication over teaching. He returned to Boyer's warning that teaching is given less and less consideration in the norms, values, and promotion and reward systems (Adler, 2016). We need to pay attention to the consequences of the POP culture on how we evaluate senior scholars. One consequence is that many universities evaluate their faculty's performance on an annual basis (Walsh, 2011). Instead, faculty should be rewarded based on programmatic research and real contributions (DeNisi, 2010).

As scholars, we should also go through a development process. Our learning process and contributions should not stop when we get our PhD or are given tenure. The standard requirements at that stage are typically that we are committed to and have acquired pedagogical skills to teach and to do research that can be published in respected journals. In the POP

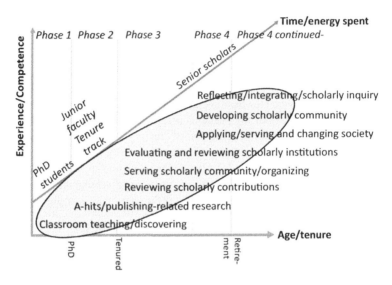

Figure 9.1   Academic knowledge

culture, at that stage we are expected to publish regularly in the highest ranked journals. Unfortunately, at present the main institutional incentive system for all scholars in most universities is to continue doing the same in all phases of their career.

However, other tasks are required in order to develop a sustainable scholarly community, and many of these can only be fulfilled by scholars with experience beyond publishing. Scholarly excellence includes knowledge and experience in serving the academic community. It includes a passion and commitment to make a difference in the academic community as well as in the world. An academic career should not only be about how many times you have been able to apply the same kind of knowledge, but should also involve continually acquiring, developing, and applying new types of knowledge—knowledge that is needed for the development of a sustainable and "true" scholarly community. I have tried to illustrate this in Figure 9.1.

The horizontal axis represents time measured in terms of age and tenure, for example the time to completing a PhD, to getting a tenured position, and to retirement. This is a typical timeline, but there may be some variations, including in the length of the intervals. The vertical axis represents experience or competences. I have sorted the different experiences/competences according to my own observations and experiences, but it should also reflect Boyer's presentations about scholarship requirements. There are variations on this dimension, but one standard for development is indicated through the circle. The circle indicates time and energy given to various scholarly tasks over the various phases of a scholarly career.

In the first phase, PhD students are typically involved in teaching, discovering, and publishing. It is a phase of formal education and training. In leading research universities or business schools, PhD students are expected to publish in premiere journals, and they are trained to do that. To get tenure in leading universities, junior faculty are required to publish regularly in such premiere journals. The second phase, the junior faculty period, can often be perceived as a publishing phase. It is in this phase that the POP label has been established. Junior faculty will not get tenure unless they are successful in their publishing efforts. Publishing in premiere journals is extremely time consuming, even if you are trained in it and have learned the techniques. However, metrics for teaching and publication have developed, and in the POP culture incentives are aligned to such measures.

Entering the third phase, PhD students and junior faculty are introduced to scholarly communities, often at conferences, and through reviewing submissions to conferences and journals. They are invited to join committees at their universities and in academic organizations, and at the time of getting tenure, some already have administrative positions at their universities or have taken on organizing or editorial roles at conferences or in journals. This kind of experience takes some professors into the area of evaluating and reviewing scholarly institutions. However, this can easily become a burnout activity, unless priorities are sorted among the fast growing demands on scholarly commitments. The activities in this phase may be visible, but comparisons across activities may be difficult. This also reflects less consistency in incentives.

The fourth phase is the least measurable. The core is neither classroom teaching, nor journal publication, nor organizational services. The fourth phase is about what you are as a scholar more than what you do as a scholar. It is about application, community development, and reflection. This phase does not stop at retirement, but will often last the rest of a scholar's life. The attributes of this phase are repeated in the AOM outgoing presidents' addresses. This is about developing and nurturing values. This is about developing a community culture based on sharing and caring; about using our time, knowledge, and energy to make a better world; and about inquiring, reflecting, and integrating to make our research important for new generations of scholars.

"Life is too short to drink bad wine." I have taken these words from Goethe as a motto, and they are increasingly important to me as the years go by. I am planning my retirement as I write this book, and I know that I do not have time to spend on things that are not important. Sharing my scholarly experiences may be a now or never matter. I need to use my time on scholarly inquiry, reflection, and integration of my various observations. I cannot postpone spending my energy on developing scholars and the scholarly community, and I cannot wait to apply my knowledge to serve and change society. Life is too short not to do the most important things.

The paradox and dilemma in Figure 9.1 are visible. If we want to stimulate true scholarship, then it may be dangerous to evaluate and incentivize senior faculty in the same way as junior faculty. The entire stock of knowledge developed over a career should be appreciated. True lifetime scholarship goes beyond publishing in premiere journals. It goes beyond serving the scholarly society through reviewing and organizing activities. Our lifelong scholarship also involves inquiry, reflection, and integration. It is about development, learning new things, and accumulating knowledge. It is not only caring for one's own tenure, but also spending time on serving our academic institutions and society in general. It is about applying our competence to serve and to change society. An academic that seeks development in the direction of true scholarship may need to prioritize among various important scholarly tasks. Our scholarly lives may go in different directions, but my reflection is that a senior scholar should spend time on doing what others cannot do.

Is this an attack on the POP culture? Yes, but I see this life cycle way of thinking not only as an attack, but also as a way of resolving the main problems with the POP culture. It is a way of displaying the challenges, and it gives directions as to how to change the system. Academy should not be characterized by neoliberal McDonaldism. Scholarship is something that should develop with maturity and experience over the entire scholarly life course. The learning process does not stop when we get our PhD.

MORE THAN ONE BOAT

In this book I have given examples from various academic associations. My main experiences have been from general academies of management such as AOM and EURAM, but also from more specialized associations such as SMS, EGOS, and IABS. I have also worked at a large number of universities and business schools in several countries. I have seen many of the challenges met by these associations. In this book, I have sorted some of my experiences from the tankship, tugboats, and lighthouses. This is about how the various associations and universities can support each other to maintain and develop vibrant communities of engaged scholars that are fostering true scholarship. To my concern, and unfortunately, I sometimes observe that these associations and universities are more concerned about their own survival and growth than on contributing to fostering true and sustainable scholarship. I wonder why it is like this.

In management research, AOM may be presented as a big tankship. I do the same in this book. For decades, AOM has been the leading global association for management scholars. Many other management associations as well as individual scholars are following in the back water of this tankship. I see the mission of AOM as serving its members and contributing to true and sustainable scholarship. It is not easy to maneuver a ship of this size in foreign waters. Long-term thinking is generally needed when sailing the global waters of academic research. The captain of the ship needs to know the consequences of maneuvering wrongly. One of the present AOM executives told me that she would prefer to sail in the Suez canal: the choices are fewer in the Suez canal than when facing options for reaching the entire world. However, the captain and the ship-owner have some alternatives, and they do not need to rely completely on their own judgment to fulfill their mission. They can get help from tugboats and split the overall mission into several sub-missions. The tugboats can help to adjust the direction of the big tankship. The shipowner can also decide to use several smaller ships and captains with specific competencies to meet parts of the overall mission. These may be local or specialized. A control center may also be established to coordinate efforts to reach the mission of the shipowner.

In their presidential addresses, several outgoing AOM presidents raised concern about the association's US-centricity developed through the global aspirations and developments of AOM. On one side, there was discussion about becoming and developing a position as the premier global academy of management. On the other side, there was discussion of becoming an international academy of management alongside other national or regional academies of management. A third position related to becoming a global academy of management, but nurturing relationships with other academies.

In this book, I have presented the role of EURAM and similar associations as tugboats that can support AOM in reaching a global ambition and charge. There is a need for local adjustments when maneuvering in international waters. Local, regional, and specialized organizations can be seen as competitors to AOM, but AOM needs high-quality collaborators and competitors that can provide local and specialized knowledge that can support AOM's overall global aspirations and charges. Good relationships among the various associations should thus be nurtured.

However, another approach can be taken. AOM can define itself as an international and welcoming US or North American-based association of management. Then it can serve its members by adapting to the needs of North American scholars and those wanting to learn from and adapt to North American values. This would be more like maneuvering in the Suez canal. While in the role of AOM's Director of International Programs (IPC) in 1998–2001, I experienced concern among many of the North American members of AOM. As AOM was moving away from being the National Academy of Management to become an international or global association, attention to US scholars' local needs disappeared. AOM has a global charge, and the direction it is taking will have global consequences. However, AOM may end up stuck in the middle, meeting the needs of neither its North American members and stakeholders, nor those in other countries or regions. This is not sustainable.

Some of the past AOM presidents warned that AOM communicated a US-centric approach to management education and research, and that the AOM journals are dominated by North American-trained scholars who share a specific model of how research should be conducted and reported (DeNisi, 2010; Hitt, 1998). Scholars in different nations evolve semi-independent intellectual traditions (Starbuck, 1999: 190). Tsui (2013: 175) thus warned that the trend toward homogenization in the research paradigm between Europe and North America and between Asia and North America is detrimental to the development of valid knowledge of contexts that are different from those of North America and Europe. Starbuck (1999: 190) was impressed by the importance of dialectic processes for intellectual development. In presenting the AOM strategic document, van de Ven (2002: 175) even argued that AOM should not seek to be a global academy of management and colonize the world. It should rather be enlightened about our global profession and confederate with associations throughout the world to accomplish this.

The AOM considers itself a global association. I can clearly see the global role the AOM plays. The AOM is a very professional association, and is influencing and setting standards for management research and scholarship. However, it is still common at AOM to identify two categories of members: ordinary members and international members, the latter being those not having strong roots in North America. When I started working with Carolyn Dexter, founder of the IPC at AOM, in 1993, I learned about her international ambitions for AOM: to raise the international awareness of North American management scholars, and for AOM to increase its "international" membership. However, at the same time, she had a passion for developing international collaborations across various associations of management, and she saw IFSAM as a meeting place for crossassociation discussions and coordination.

Is IFSAM still a possible coordinator or collaboration across various academies of management? In his presidential address, DeNisi (2010) raised warnings about having AOM in a global leadership position. He argued that we need to connect to the world around us, and that we cannot assume that the world would want AOM to be leaders in a global consortium. I believe that in the future AOM will be considered as the American Academy of Management. That makes it important to define the kind of relationships AOM wishes to have with other associations of management. I do not think that other associations of management, for example EURAM, ANZAM, EGOS, or SMS, will wish only to act as tugboats and define their main role as "supporter of AOM." They will have their own objectives and identities. When I was EURAM president, I initiated coordination activities that did not lean on AOM dominance. However, I do not think that EURAM shall take this coordinating role. I will like to give IFSAM or similar federations important roles in coordination among learned societies on the global arena.

I believe that when our scholarly associations stand together, we can make a change. However, we must contribute to collaboration and not to competition.

WHERE TO NAVIGATE—LIGHTHOUSES

In this book I have presented several "lighthouses" that help us navigate the journey to true scholarship, returning to meaning, and resolving the crisis in research. The work of Boyer is one of these lighthouses, and we see several associations and scholars standing up and seeking to show us the way. The presidential addresses of the outgoing AOM presidents are further such lighthouses (Chapter 3). I highly value these contributions. I do want to see more institutions, universities, and business schools standing out as lighthouses. There are currently a few, for example those that have signed DORA or endorsed RRBM. On an individual basis, I have placed a sign outside my office door stating that I am a signatory of DORA. I think it is important that we individually show that we are taking a stand.

In Chapter 7, I presented a university as an example of a lighthouse. My late career experience from Witten/Herdecke University (UW/H) in some ways acted as a philosophical lighthouse that helped me sort and navigate among many scholarly values. I was highly appreciative of what I was learning about UW/H's roots in anthroposophical and Humboldtian traditions. I found UW/H to have the features of a lighthouse in showing the direction for true scholarship. This scholarship goes beyond learning the tricks of the trade or cracking the codes to publish. It is holistic, and we cannot make a split between our scholarly lives and us as private persons. True scholarship is about who we are. It is our lives.

Bartunek, in her presidential address, presented her dreams for the future. It was a dream about how the AOM has the resources to support the profession in making a positive difference in the world. She also urged us to "develop, in doctoral students, an awareness that research findings and new ways of conceptualizing can and should make a dif-ference for good in the world" (Bartunek, 2003: 202). Other outgoing AOM presidents wanted us to dare to care and even fight for what we believe in. Tsui (2013: 177) invited "all to accept the compassion pledge by summoning the courage to conduct research that inspires managers to lead compassionately, to teach in ways that lead our students to act justly, to help our young colleagues make a difference, and to serve in ways that lead to a better Academy and a better world."

It may be a challenge to train and mentor PhD students and junior faculty. There is a need to communicate both long and short-term issues and training at the same time. In Witten, I tried to instill in the junior scholars the desire to make a difference. I wanted them to become social scholars and combine their short-term survival training with a heart for people and compassion for others. During my time as a student in the 1970s, I was involved in a religious organization that had a motto taken from the Bible: "And the things you have heard me say in the presence of many witnesses entrust to reliable people who will also be qualified to teach others."[1] I think this motto sets out a principle I still wish to keep to.

I now define my scholarly role as that of a mentor. I still urgently try to show PhD students and junior faculty what true scholarship may be about, but at the same time I try to help them survive in a POP culture—to help them become tenured. I presented some examples of this work in Chapters 6, 7, and 8. I wanted to include them in a community described by a sharing philosophy that is communal, open, and impact-driven. It is a culture focusing on second and third-order impacts. This is also what I want to communicate to the readers of this book. Life is too short not to do what is most important.

---

[1] Letter from Paul to Timothy, chapter 2, verse 2: https://www.biblica.com/bible/niv/2-timothy/2/

10. A sharing philosophy—changing the game

Ritorno al passato and "Life is too short to drink bad wine" have been the two mottos driving me while writing this book about a "sharing philosophy" for scholarship and research. *Ritorno al passato* is about reflections about the past, while "life is too short to drink bad wine" is about what we do to meet the future. I have developed this book through an introspective approach in which I build on the role of my own experiences in interpreting the present situation, the needs it creates, and future actions. I present in this book the creation of a sharing philosophy for resolving the crisis in research and changing the game. This philosophy is driven by open innovation, collectivity, and impact. It is led by a drive for relevance and meaning. However, it goes beyond relevance. Knowledge is developed in open systems, through diversity and in interactions with a large set of stakeholders. It goes beyond individual credit for publishing in premiere journals. I present this philosophy as a new game, and my ambition is to change the existing "publish or perish" one.

The ambitions, realities, and illustrations in this book go beyond management research. They may also go beyond research in social sciences, into humanities and natural sciences. In most disciplines we struggle with the presence of a "publish or perish" culture that takes us away from true scholarship. However, my experience is of management research, and the book is embedded in a management research context. It has also been influenced by my own experiences, and it is written in a form representing introspections and my own reflections. Furthermore, the book is influenced by reflections from past presidents of the Academy of Management (AOM) and Boyer's work on true scholarship. It is influenced by several recent initiatives and contributions, for example from the San Francisco Declaration (DORA), Responsible Research in Business and Management (RRBM), Open Science, scholars such as Mats Alvesson and Andrew Pettigrew, and my many friends and colleagues.

In the first part of the book—Chapters 2, 3, 4, and 5—I introduced an ecosystem thinking for changing the present 'publish or perish' culture in academia. Returning to true scholarship, as described by Boyer, for example, was the objective. I presented an ecosystem with five main elements: institutions, audience, message, channels, and community. I presented the state of the art, scholarly ambitions, and change initiatives for each of the elements.

The ecosystem approach has a focus on joint and coordinated efforts among many actors related to the various elements in the system. Scholars in many disciplines have identified the urgent problems with the present academic "publish or perish" culture. My contribution goes beyond presenting the "publish and perish" problem (Moosa, 2018), the "state of the misery" (Alvesson, Gabriel, and Paulsen, 2017), and the crisis in management studies (Tourish, 2019). I present and summarize ways to take action in a scholarly ecosystem framework. Several important initiatives are taken, but the ecosystem presentation calls for synchronization of these actions. My first contribution through this book is to sort the discussion in the ecosystem framework, and thus show the importance of individual as well as common and synchronized contributions.

In the second part of the book—Chapters 6, 7, and 8—I presented and illustrated the sharing philosophy of scholarship and of doing research. This goes beyond Boyer's description of the functions of scholarship. I presented experiences of the scholarly community, of scholarly values, and of making an impact. The focus in this part was more about what scholars are than what scholars do. The sharing philosophy stands out as a contrast to an individualistic publish or perish culture. The sharing philosophy is communal, open, and impact-driven. In the second part of the book I presented examples of ways to achieve this open philosophy, and showed how many of the suggestions presented in the first part can be applied in practice.

In Chapter 9, I concluded with some summarizing reflections. The first was a life cycle perspective on our scholarship and scholarly activities. During our long scholarly lives we should develop and learn, and we should not spend our time and energy on exactly the same tasks we undertook as PhD students or junior faculty. We should continue to develop our knowledge and give priority to tasks that nobody else can do. "Life is too short to drink bad wine." Senior scholars should spend time on scholarly inquiry by reflecting and integrating, should devote their time to developing junior scholars and the scholarly community, and should apply their experience to serve and change society—for a better world. Our institutions, including our universities and business schools, should facilitate such activities through their support and incentive systems. Senior scholars are today often punished for spending their time using the voice they have developed over their scholarly lifetime.

A second reflection is about the role of our scholarly associations. They need to appreciate that we have context specific charges and needs. We need to appreciate diversity among associations, to meet both local and specific needs, but semi-independent intellectual traditions should be the background for important intellectual processes. These may also contribute to adjusting the direction of the big professional tankships.

Third, I reflected on the importance of champions, benchmarks, examples, and lighthouses. Individual scholars can be important role models for other scholars. We should take a stand, commit to it, and set an example as to how to follow up. I would like scholars in general to sign the San Francisco Declaration (DORA), and management scholars to endorse the Responsible Research in Business and Management (RRBM) initiatives. Our universities and business schools should take a lead on the "return to meaning" and "true scholarship" instead of adapting to the existing publish or perish culture. We need lighthouses among our universities.

My final reflection is about our commitment to serve each other. We should commit to developing a sharing philosophy of research and to creating a new game. In this book I have presented a sharing philosophy that is communal, open, and impact-driven. We should channel our competencies and experiences into caring for and supporting others so that they also become skilled and motivated to do the same.

What, then, are the main contributions of this book for changing the game? From my perspective, they are as follows:

- The first contribution is to place the discussion about crisis in scholarship in an ecosystem framework, and show the importance of individual as well as synchronized contributions.
- The second contribution is to present a new game by illustrating a "sharing philosophy" of scholarship and of doing research.
- A third contribution is to recognize the need to appreciate diversity among associations, to meet both local and specific needs, as well as the contributions of semi-independent intellectual traditions to important intellectual processes.
- Finally, we need institutional and individual champions, role models, and benchmarks. We need lighthouses.

References

Adler, N.J., & Harzing, A.W. (2009). When knowledge wins: Transcending the sense and nonsense of academic rankings. *Academy of Management Learning & Education*, 8(1): 72–95.

Adler, P.S. (2016). 2015 Presidential address: Our teaching mission. *Academy of Management Review*, 41(2): 185–95.

Aguinis, H., Shapiro, D.L., Antonacopoulou, E.P., & Cummings, T.G. (2014). Scholarly impact: A pluralist conceptualization. *Academy of Management Learning & Education*, 13(4): 623–39.

Altbach, P.G. (2004). Globalisation and the university: Myths and realities in an unequal world. *Tertiary Education & Management*, 10(1): 3–25.

Alvesson, M., & Gabriel, Y. (2013). Beyond formulaic research: In praise of greater diversity in organizational research and publications. *Academy of Management Learning & Education*, 12(2): 245–63.

Alvesson, M., Gabriel, Y., & Paulsen, R. (2017). *Return to meaning: A social science with something to say*. Oxford: Oxford University Press.

Alvesson, M., & Sandberg, J. (2013). Has management studies lost its way? Ideas for more imaginative and innovative research. *Journal of Management Studies*, 50(1): 128–52.

Alvesson, M., & Sköldberg, K. (2017). *Reflexive methodology: New vistas for qualitative research*. Thousand Oaks, CA: Sage.

Bartunek, J.M. (2003). A dream for the academy. *Academy of Management Review*, 28(2): 198–203.

Bartunek, J.M. (2007). Academic–practitioner collaboration need not require joint or relevant research: Toward a relational scholarship of integration. *Academy of Management Journal*, 50(6): 1323–33.

Bartunek, J.M. (2014). Introduction: Bringing to life a correlation of .14: Teaching evidence-based management engagingly and convincingly. *Academy of Management Learning & Education*, 13(1): 102–3.

Bartunek, J.M., & Rynes, S.L. (2014). Academics and practitioners are alike and unlike: The paradoxes of academic–practitioner relationships. *Journal of Management*, 40(5): 1181–201.

Baruch, Y. (2013). Careers in academe: The academic labor market as an eco-system. *Career Development International*, 18(2): 196–210.

Bilimoria, D., & Huse, M. (1997). A qualitative comparison of the boardroom experiences of US and Norwegian women corporate directors. *International Review of Women and Leadership*, 3(2): 63–76.

Boyer, E.L. (1990). *Scholarship reconsidered: Priorities of the professoriate*. Lawrenceville, NJ: Princeton University Press.

Boyer, E.L. (1996a). From scholarship reconsidered to scholarship assessed. *Quest*, 48(2):129–39.

Boyer, E.L. (1996b). The scholarship of engagement. *Bulletin of the American Academy of Arts and Sciences*, 49(7): 18–33 (also published in *Journal of Public Service and Outreach*, 1: 11–20).

Cern, K.C. (2013). *Boyer's four domains of scholarship critically reassessed*, paper prepared as a part of European Commission's 7th framework program grant EduWel, Adam Mickiewics University, Poznan, Poland.

Chen, M.J. (2014). Presidential address—Becoming ambicultural: A personal quest, and aspiration for organizations. *Academy of Management Review*, 39(2): 119–37.

Cummings, T.G. (2007). Quest for an engaged academy. *Academy of Management Review*, 32(2): 355–60.

Cunliffe, A.L., & Scaratti, G. (2017). Embedding impact in engaged research: Developing socially useful knowledge through dialogical sensemaking. *British Journal of Management*, 28(1): 29–44.

Davis, G.F. (2015). Editorial essay: What is organizational research for? *Administrative Science Quarterly*, 60(2): 179–88.

DeNisi, A.S. (2010). 2009 Presidential address: Challenges and opportunities for the academy in the next decade. *Academy of Management Review*, 35(2): 190–201.

DORA, n.d. https://sfdora.org/. Accessed Feb. 21, 2019.

Eisenhardt, K.M., Graebner, M.E., & Sonenshein, S. (2016). Grand challenges and inductive methods: Rigor without rigor mortis. *Academy of Management Journal*, 59(4): 1113–23.

Etzioni, A. (1959). Authority structure and organizational effectiveness. *Administrative Science Quarterly*, 41(1): 43–67.

Ferraro, F., Etzion, D., & Gehman, J. (2015). Tackling grand challenges pragmatically: Robust action revisited. *Organization Studies*, 36(3): 363–90.

Gabrielsson, J., & Huse, M. (2002). The accumulation of knowledge of boards of directors—Contributions from 100 student reports. *Conference paper presented at the 2nd EURAM conference on innovative research in management in Stockholm*.

Gabrielsson, J., & Huse, M. (2004). Context, behavior, and evolution: Challenges in research on boards and governance. *International Studies of Management & Organization*, 34(2): 11–36.

George, G., Howard-Grenville, J., Joshi, A., & Tihanyi, L. (2016). Understanding and tackling societal grand challenges through management research. *Academy of Management Journal*, 59(6): 1880–95.

Glynn, M.A. (2019). 2018 presidential address: The mission of community and the promise of collective action. *Academy of Management Review*, 44(2): 244–53.

Guerin, C. (2013). Rhizomatic research cultures, writing groups and academic researcher identities. *International Journal of Doctoral Studies*, 8: 137–50.

Hakim, C. (2011). *Erotic capital: The power of attraction in the boardroom and the bedroom*. New York: Basic Books.

Hall, J., & Martin, B.R. (2019). Towards a taxonomy of research misconduct: The case of business school research. *Research Policy*, 48(2): 414–27.

Hambrick, D.C. (1994). What if the academy actually mattered? *Academy of Management Review*, 19(1): 11–16.

Hill, P.A. (2010) Twenty years on: Ernest Boyer, scholarship and the scholarship of teaching. *Paper presented at the American University of Beirut, Hamra, Lebanon.*

Hitt, M.A. 1998. Twenty-first-century organizations: Business firms, business schools, and the academy. *Academy of Management Review*, 23(2): 218–24.

Hodgkinson, G.P., Herriot, P., & Anderson, N. (2001). Re-aligning the stakeholders in management research: Lessons from industrial, work and organizational psychology. *British Journal of Management*, 12: S41–S48.

Hodgkinson, G.P., & Rousseau, D.M. (2009). Bridging the rigour–relevance gap in management research: It's already happening! *Journal of Management Studies*, 46(3): 534–46.

Hodgkinson, G.P., & Starkey, K. (2011). Not simply returning to the same answer over and over again: Reframing relevance. *British Journal of Management*, 22(3): 355–69.

Honig, B., & Lampel, J. (2018). Reflections on scientific misconduct in management: Unfortunate incidents or a normative crisis? *Academy of Management Perspectives*, 32(4): 412–42.

Honig, B., Lampel, J., Siegel, D., & Drnevich, P. (2017). Special section on ethics in management research: Norms, identity, and community in the 21st century. *Academy of Management Learning & Education*, 16(1): 84–93.

Huff, A.S. 2000. 1999 presidential address: Changes in organizational knowledge production. *Academy of Management Review*, 25(2): 288–93.

Huse, M. (1993). *Tante, barbar eller klan: Om styrets rolle,* Bodø: Nordland Research Institute.

Huse, M. (1995). *Stakeholder perspectives on corporate governance: A sample of Scandinavian contributions*. Bodø: Nordland Research Institute.

Huse, M. (1996). Researching unresearchable issues: Ethical dilemmas in qualitative research. *Proceedings of the International Association for Business and Society*, 7: 853–63.

Huse, M. (1998). Researching the dynamics of board–stakeholder relations. *Long Range Planning*, 31(2): 218–26.

Huse, M. (2007). *Boards, governance and value creation: The human side of corporate governance.* Cambridge: Cambridge University Press.

Huse, M. (ed.). (2008a). *The value creating board: Corporate governance and organizational behaviour*. Abingdon: Routledge.

Huse, M. (2008b). Building blocks in understanding behavioural perspectives of boards: developing a research stream. In Huse (ed.) *The value creating board: Corporate governance and organizational behaviour* (pp.72–83). Abingdon: Routledge.

Huse, M. (2008c). Exploring methods and concepts in studies of board processes. In Huse (ed.) *The value creating board: Corporate governance and organizational behaviour* (pp.221–33). Abingdon: Routledge.

Huse, M. (2008d). The "value creating board" surveys: A benchmark. In Huse (ed.) *The value creating board: Corporate governance and organizational behaviour* (pp.367–83). Abingdon: Routledge.

Huse, M. (2010). Building a community of engaged scholars. *European Management Review*, 7: 133–5.

Huse, M. (2011). The golden skirts: Changes in board composition following gender quotas on corporate boards. *Presented at the Australian and New Zealand Academy Meeting in Wellington, NZ.*

Huse, M. (2012a). Letter from the president, *EURAM newsletter* 51(June): 1–3.

Huse, M. (2012b). The "golden skirts": Lessons from Norway about women on corporate boards of directors. In Gröschl, S. & Takagi, J. (eds) *Diversity Quotas, Diverse Perspectives* (pp.11–23). Gower/Ashgate, republished 2016, Abingdon: Routledge.

Huse, M. (2015). Kjønn i styrer: Verden ser til Norge. In Alsos. G., Bjørkhaug, H., Bolsø, A., & Ljunggren, E. (eds) *Kjønn og næringsliv i Norge* (pp.153–74). Oslo: Cappelen.

Huse, M. (2018a). *Value-creating boards: Challenges for future research and practice.* Cambridge: Cambridge University Press.

Huse, M. (2018b). Gender in the Boardroom: Learnings from world-leader Norway. *FACTBase Bulletin 58.* Committee for Perth/University of Western Australia.

Huse, M. (2019). What matters most for our scholarly community: Reflections from former AOM presidents. In Benito, R. and Lunnan, R. (eds) *Voyages of a scholar: Navigating companies, channels, and clusters* (pp.21–44). Bergen: Fagbokforlaget.

Huse, M., & Solberg, A.G. (2006). Gender-related boardroom dynamics: How Scandinavian women make and can make contributions on corporate boards. *Women in Management Review*, 21(2): 113–30.

Ireland, R.D. (2015). 2014 presidential address: Our academy, our future. *Academy of Management Review*, 40(2): 151–62.

Jackson, S.E. (2012). WE@ AOM. *Academy of Management Review*, 37(2): 170–71.

Kogut, B. (2008). Rankings, schools, and final reflections on ideas and taste. *European Management Review*, 5(4): 191–4.

Kraker, P., Leony, D., Reinhardt, W., & Beham, G. (2011). The case for an open science in technology enhanced learning. *International Journal of Technology Enhanced Learning*, 3(6): 643–54.

Kruse, O. (2006). The origins of writing in the disciplines: Traditions of seminar writing and the Humboldtian ideal of the research university. *Written Communication*, 23(3): 331–52.

Lee, T.W. (2009). The management professor. *Academy of Management Review*, 34(2): 196–9.

Levin, K., Cashore, B., Bernstein, S., & Auld, G. (2012). Overcoming the tragedy of super wicked problems: Constraining our future selves to ameliorate global climate change. *Policy Sciences*, 45(2): 123–52.

Machold, S., Huse, M., Hansen, K., & Brogi, M. (eds). (2013). *Getting women on to corporate boards: A snowball starting in Norway.* Cheltenham: Edward Elgar Publishing.

MacIntosh, R., Beech, N., Bartunek, J., Mason, K., Cooke, B., & Denyer, D. (2017). Impact and management research: Exploring relationships between temporality, dialogue, reflexivity and praxis. *British Journal of Management*, 28(1): 3–13.

McGahan, A.M. (2018). 2017 presidential address—Freedom in scholarship: Lessons from Atlanta. *Academy of Management Review*, 42(2): 173–8.

Mintzberg, H. (1979). *The structuring of organizations*. Englewood Cliffs: Prentice-Hall.

Moosa, I.A. 2018. *Publish or perish: Perceived benefits versus unintended consequences*. Cheltenham: Edward Elgar Publishing.

Mowday, R.T. (1997). Reaffirming our scholarly values. *Academy of Management Review*, 22(2): 335–45.

Olssen, M., & Peters, M.A. (2005). Neoliberalism, higher education and the knowledge economy: From the free market to knowledge capitalism. *Journal of Education Policy*, 20(3): 313–45.

Özbilgin, M.F. (2009). From journal rankings to making sense of the world. *Academy of Management Learning & Education*, 8(1): 113–21.

Pearce, J.L. (2004). What do we know and how do we really know it? *Academy of Management Review*, 29(2): 175–9.

Pettigrew, A.M. (2011). Scholarship with impact. *British Journal of Management*, 22(3): 347–54.

Rennison, B.W. (2012). *Knæk kønnets koder: Kvinder i ledelse*. Copenhagen: Gyldendal A/S.

Rigolini, A., & Huse, M. (2019). Women and multiple board memberships: Social capital and institutional pressure. *Journal of Business Ethics*, online first https://doi.org/10.1007/s10551-019-04313-6

Romme, A.G.L., Avenier, M.J., Denyer, D., Hodgkinson, G.P., Pandza, K., Starkey, K., & Worren, N. (2015). Towards common ground and trading zones in management research and practice. *British Journal of Management*, 26(3): 544–59.

Rousseau, D.M. (2006). Is there such a thing as evidence-based management? *Academy of Management Review*, 31(2): 256–69.

RRBM (2017). A vision of responsible research in business and management: Striving for useful and credible knowledge. *RRBM position paper of 22 November 2017*, https://rrbm.network/. Accessed Mar. 3, 2019.

Rynes, S.L., Bartunek, J.M., & Daft, R.L. (2001). Across the great divide: Knowledge creation and transfer between practitioners and academics. *Academy of Management Journal*, 44(2): 340–55.

Sandberg, S. (2013). *Lean In: Women, Work and the Will to Lead*. London: WH Allen.

Scott, C.E. (2019). The crisis in academic research, RRBM Blog, January 12, https://rrbm.network/the-crisis-in-academic-researchcarole-e-scott/. Accessed Jan. 12, 2019.

Sealy, R., Doldor, E., Vinnicombe, S., Terjesen, S., Anderson, D., & Atewologun, D. (2017). Expanding the notion of dialogic trading zones for impactful research: The case of women on boards research. *British Journal of Management*, 28(1): 64–83.

Seierstad, C., Warner-Søderholm, G., Torchia, M., & Huse, M. (2017). Increasing the number of women on boards: The role of actors and processes. *Journal of Business Ethics*, 141(2): 289–315.

Shapiro, D. (2017). Making the academy full voice-meaningful. *Academy of Management Review*, 42(2): 165–73.

Smith, K.G. (2008). Fighting the orthodoxy: Learning to be pragmatic. *Academy of Management Review*, 33(2): 304–8.

Starbuck, W.H. (1999). Our shrinking earth. *Academy of Management Review*, 24(2): 187–90.

Starbuck, W.H. (2005). How much better are the most prestigious journals? The statistics of academic publication. *Organization Science*, 16: 180–200.

Starkey, K., Hatchuel, A., & Tempest, S. (2004). Rethinking the business school. *Journal of Management Studies*, 41(8): 1521–31.

Starkey, K., Hatchuel, A., & Tempest, S. (2009). Management research and the new logic of discovery and engagement. *Journal of Management Studies*, 46(3): 547–58.

Starkey, K., & Madan, P. (2001). Bridging the relevance gap: Aligning stakeholders in the future of management research. *British Journal of Management*, 12: S3–S26.

Tourish, D. (2019). *Management studies in crisis: Fraud, deception and meaningless research.* Cambridge: Cambridge University Press.

Tsui, A.S. (2004). Contributing to global management knowledge: A case for high quality indigenous research. *Asia Pacific Journal of Management*, 21(4): 491–513.

Tsui, A.S. (2013). 2012 presidential address—On compassion in scholarship: Why should we care? *Academy of Management Review*, 38(2): 167–80.

Tsui, A.S. (2018). Commentary on "opportunities and challenges of engaged indigenous scholarship (Vand de Ven, Meyer, and Jing, 2018)." *Management and Organization Review*, 14(3): 463–6.

Tung, R.L. (2005). Reflections on engendering a sustainable community within the Academy. *Academy of Management Review*, 30(2): 239–44.

Uhl-bien, M., Sitkin, S., & Rynes, S. (2018). Responsible research call to action: Improving lives by improving research impact—Research–practice partnership, *RRBM handout, AOM Chicago*.

Uhrmacher, P.B. (1995). Uncommon schooling: A historical look at Rudolf Steiner, anthroposophy, and Waldorf education. *Curriculum Inquiry*, 25(4): 381–406.

Van De Ven, A.H. (2002). Strategic directions for the Academy of Management: This academy is for you! *Academy of Management Review*, 27(2): 171–84.

Van De Ven, A.H. (2011). Building a European community of engaged scholars. *European Management Review*, 8(4): 189–95.

Von Glinow, M.A. (1996). 1995 presidential address: On minority rights and majority accommodations. *Academy of Management Review*, 21(2): 346–50.

Walsh, J.P. (2011). Presidential address: Embracing the sacred in our secular scholarly world. *Academy of Management Review*, 36(2): 215–34.

Wells, P., & Nieuwenhuis, P. (2017). Operationalizing deep structural sustainability in business: Longitudinal immersion as extensive engaged scholarship. *British Journal of Management*, 28(1): 45–63.

Whetten, D.A. (2001). What matters most. *Academy of Management Review*, 26(2): 175–8.

Wilson, D., & McKiernan, P. (2011). Global mimicry: Putting strategic choice back on the business school agenda. *British Journal of Management*, 22(3): 457–69.

Winter, R. (2011). A call for critical perspectives in qualitative research. *Forum Qualitative Sozialforschung/Forum: Qualitative Social Research*, 12(1): Art. 7.

Wright, R.P., & Brown, K.G. (2014). *Educating tomorrow's thought-leaders: Distinguished scholars answer a burning question.* Strategic Management Society: Teaching Community.

Zheng, C., & Kouwenberg, R. (2019). A bibliometric review of global research on corporate governance and board attributes. *Sustainability*, 11(12): 3428. doi:10.3390/su11123428

Index

Printed and bound by CPI Group (UK) Ltd, Croydon, CR0 4YY

23/04/2025

14660982-0003